EXPORT PROMOTION IN INDIA
–A Strategic Perspective

EXPORT PROMOTION IN INDIA

—A Strategic Perspective

Dr. Balan Satchit

Commonwealth

EXPORT PROMOTION IN INDIA

Ist Edition : 1999
ISBN 81-7169-547-7

Published by :
Ajay Verma
Commonwealth Publishers
4831/24, Prahlad Street,
Ansari Road, Darya Ganj,
New Delhi - 110002
Phone : 3272541, 3257835
Fax : 91-011-3257835

Laser Typesetting by :
Stylish Laser Typesetter,
Delhi

Printed at :
Roshan offset
Delhi.

PREFACE

Having been introduced to the fascinating world of foreign trade way back in 1975 and subsequently associated with export, both as a businessman in Hong Kong as well as a teacher of International Business, the field of international trade had retained its attraction through most of my career. During the business years, in the early 1980s, my attempts at exporting products from India had to face many procedural, technical as well as logistic problems especially in areas like shipment schedules, quality standards and lack of market orientation. This was in contrast to my experiences in Taiwan, Hong Kong and Thailand. What was found particularly lacking was the right approach in addition to problems with bureaucracy and organisational inefficiency. It was often forgotten that the foreign buyer is least concerned about the ideological, political, social or infrastructural problems faced by the exporter in India. For the buyer, the most important factor is delivery of the merchandise as promised, in a quality as agreed and acceptable to his consumers without any delay or unnecessary hassle.

Against this background, I could not have found an area of research more relevant to my experience and interest. This study has been the beginning of a continuing research in Export Development and Foreign Direct Investment, both of which are likely to be twin pillars on which a healthy Indian economy has to be built.

Chapter one introduces the study and the special reasons why export promotion has assumed such importance since the early 90s and emphasises the need to develop exports to combat the many economic problems facing the country. Briefly, the importance, objective, scope and limitations of the study are discussed.

The second chapter paints the background of the study, the direction and composition of India's foreign trade today. To gain a clear picture of India's export/import trade, one has to go back a few centuries when India was well known around the world for the products she could export. The historical background also helps to identify the events which shaped the composition of India's exports and how her foreign trade was influenced by the industrial revolution and structure of the UK industry. The chapter also views the foreign trade scenario through Independence and partition as well as the five decades since Independence up to the period following the reforms.

Countries of the developing world, including India face several trade barriers—both tariff and non-tariff. While tariffs in the developed markets are low and are being further lowered, the non-tariff barriers pose a stronger impediment. Chapter three examines the barriers in general and the non-tariff barriers in particular which India is facing in its major markets. An attempt has also been made to examine the possible impact of the WTO, SAPTA, EU, NAFTA, ASEAN and APEC on India's exports, and to find an answer to the question whether India should join a trading bloc.

Globalisation being an ongoing trend, is bound to impact India's foreign trade as well as the structure of its domestic market. Closer home, the South Asian economies have agreed to preferential trade amongst them with the ultimate goal of setting up a South Asian Free Trade Area. In addition to ASEAN, unofficial growth zones are developing in South East Asia which have to be targeted for development of India's exports, as discussed under chapter four.

Both developed and developing countries do promote exports through multifarious programs. An examination of such programs around the world would reveal that India has in it books, almost all similar programs. The East Asian economies have recorded substantial growth in their economies through exports and this process has been referred to as miracle. Can India follow them and bring about a miracle? How much of the East Asian strategies could be adopted and adapted by India? Chapter five seeks to find answers for these.

Liberalisation or reforms of the Indian economy since 1991 has left an imprint on the export performance. Several countries world wide had attempted liberalisation at different times with varying intensities, meeting with different levels of success. Liberalisation has its proponents as well as opponents and widely differing views on liberalisation has been included in chapter six. Though it is too early to judge the efficacy of the new economic reforms, exports recorded between 1991 and 1996 are gratifying, though the next phase has been less than encouraging.

Chapter seven reviews the export promotion strategies under different heads such as finance, insurance, institutional framework, state trading, etc., adding suggestions for a more efficient execution of the strategies. A few important export sectors like gems and jewellery, software, garments, etc. are examined followed by a closer view of the more important markets for India—both current and future.

In the light of discussions in earlier chapters, chapter eight tries to evolve a future model of Export Strategy in India, by examining proposals by Board ot Trade, ASSOCHAM, FICCI and Commerce Ministry of Government of India. Future direction of exports based on a focused strategy and the products as well as the markets being targeted for special attention are briefly studied.

The concluding chapter nine tries to hypothesise the major causes for India's less than spectacular growth in exports. Among the causes identified are the domestic orientation of Indian industry, the inability to consistently meet international quality standards, hesitance by many entrepreneurs to venture into exports and inadequate infrastructure and productive inefficiency of the domestic sector. Recommendations for short, medium and long term policy considerations are included in chapter nine which also looks at future achievable targets.

With a fast changing international business environment, research needs to be continuous and consistent over periods of time. This researcher hopes to continue his study of twin areas which are crucial to India's development—foreign trade and foreign direct investment and fervently hopes that support and encouragement as in the past would be forthcoming. A research work, such as the current one perhaps could not have been possible without the encouragement, guidance, direction, comments and friendly criticism from very many sources, both institutions and individuals too numerous to list. I look back with gratitude to them for being the recipient of all above.

Balan Satchit

CONTENTS

List of Tables and Figures

List of Abbreviations

ACP	African, Carribean and Pacific Countries
ASEAN	Association of South East Asian Nations
ADB	Asian Development Bank
APEC	Asia Pacific Economic Co-operation
BOP	Balance of Payments
BOT	Balance of Trade
EU	European Union
GDP	Gross Domestic Product
GNP	Gross National Product
IDA	International Development Association
IFC	International Finance Corporation
IBRD	International Bank for Reconstruction and Development
ILO	International Labour Office
IMF	International Monetary Fund
MFA	Multi Fibre Arrangement
NIC	Newly Industrialised Countries
NAFTA	North American Free Trade Agreement
NTB	Non-Tariff Barriers
OECD	Organisation for Economic Cooperation and Development

OPEC	Organisation of Petroleum Exporting Countries
PRC	The People's Republic of China
QRs	Quantitative Restrictions
SAARC	South Asian Association for Regional Co-operation
SAPTA	South Asian Preferential Trade Agreement
SAFTA	South Asian Free Trade Area
UKCC	United Kingdom Commercial Corporation
WTO	World Trade Organisation

Chapter 1

Introduction and Methodology Used

1.1 INTRODUCTION

At no time in the history of India had export assumed such an important role as it did in 1990. With hardly enough foreign exchange to pay for two week's imports, decreasing aid support, risk of default on debt repayments looming large, a fiscal deficit that was constantly growing wider—there was no other option but to go in for liberalisation. And one of the effective tools to combat the balance of trade problem was to embark on a path to revitalise the export trade.

Increasing globalisation of world markets has led to enormous growth in international trade (estimated at USD 9890 billion with export constituting over USD 4875 billion in 1995). The South East Asian economies estimated to be the fastest growing region in the world, have a 23% share of world exports. The experience of the first line of tigers or NIC's in Asia (Hong Kong, Taiwan, South Korea and Singapore) is being repeated by the second line of tigers—Malaysia, Thailand and Indonesia- perhaps to be followed by a third wave including Vietnam. In contrast, the developing nations of Africa and South America had been struggling to come out of cycles of slow export growth.

Large developing countries like Brazil, China and India saw their export growth limited during the fifties.

But China's (PRC) four modernisations since 1978 had proved that with commitment and concerted effort, a developing country can record remarkable export growth.

In their quest for increasing exports, countries have been developing export promotion strategies of various descriptions. And competitively too, so many a player in export has to pursue more and more attractive and dynamic strategies to support exports, or else be left out of the race for the world's markets.

The increasing globalisation has prompted even countries like Myanmar to open up their market and try to come out of isolation. India which has a long history of export trade cannot but get over it's complacence as it's share of world exports has decelerated to 0.64% in 94-95 (-estimate) from 1.05% in the early sixties and take it's rightful place in world trade.

The economic reforms since 1991 have attracted foreign investments from around the world, and if the investments are to be benefited from, export growth has to be substantial and befitting the size and structure of a country of 920 million. The success in export alone will help ameliorate the problems of unemployment, poverty and illiteracy and poor standard of living.

All the above factors point to the need to look objectively at India's export performance—the areas which have been successful to some extent and those not successful with a view to redrawing the country's export promotion strategy.

The strategies of successful countries, big and small need to be evaluated for adaptation, and adoption and to arrive at a well considered, flexible and practical export promotion strategy for the future. Of course many of the strategies successful elsewhere may have little relevance to the political, social, cultural and economic environment of today's India. But they point out the need for commitment from Government and business in promotion of exports.

Economic integration around the world- (NAFTA, EU, APEC, and ASEAN), the increasing protectionism it may pose to non-members, the influence of WTO—and several other geo-political changes in the area of international trade may constrain the freedom of choice in strategies. But India has to play by the rules of international trade, if it aims to be an important player in international trade.

India has no time to lose—it is imperative that active development of export strategy has to be taken up and it is gratifying to note that the Government of India and of late the state governments have taken this up for focused attention. While the businessmen are likely to have a relatively shorter term view and the Government subject to political and industrial lobbies, the academia has to come forward to participate in developing or suggesting a long term , unbiased and objective criterion for export promotion. And this should be the contribution of academia to nation building.

1.2 PRIOR RESEARCH AND LITERATURE REVIEW

Research on foreign trade is considered vital for laying down policies and "has a long term objective to facilitate planning for exports on an objective basis by way of identification of sectors with relatively larger comparative advantage and directing investment and other efforts to such sectors" (Mr. K.G. Vaidya, Ministry of Foreign Trade, Government of India). Mr. N.V. Rangaswamy of the IIFT emphasized the objectives as :

- To collect all relevant information.
- To suggest action oriented recommendations which can withstand commercial judgement.

- To fill in the gaps in the required information by way of further research.

The area of export research is wide and varied and, in the Indian context, encompasses terms of payment, product development, visible and invisible trade barriers, market studies and marketing strategies in importing countries. Export research is often grouped under internal and external research (again divided into area research, commodity research, policy research and price research).

In India, a host of agencies are engaged in export research to aid the export promotion drive, they are :

- Export Promotion Councils : All 20 export promotion councils carry out continuous research in their specific are as of interest.
- Commodity Boards : All nine commodity boards are engaged in export research.
  EDAs
  ITPO
- Trade Authorities : Trade fair centres, marine products, agriculture, etc.
- Public Sector Trading Corporations : STC, MMTC, etc.
- Financial Institutions : Commercial Banks, ECGC, Exim Bank, Chambers of Commerce, PHDCCI, FICCI, ASSOCHAM, Indian Jute Mills Association, Universities and Research Institutes, IIMs, National Council of Applied Economic Research, Administrative Staff College, Indian Institute of Packaging and Indian Institute of Foreign Trade.

A special mention has to be made of IIFT which has pioneered research in export since its inception in 1964, especially on overseas market surveys, country studies, market potential surveys and functional research. Areas researched by IIFT include protectionism, non-tariff barriers, cooperation with Asian economies, etc. Several seminars have also been organised by the Institute contributing to expertise in this area.

Attempts at identifying areas of research on export promotion strategies was met with limited success as no specific research work focussing on export promotion *per se* could be traced though export promotion has been studied as part of country and area studies. Primarily export research has been aimed at practical day-to-day issues rather than taking a multi faceted longer term approach.

This research tries to synthesize the thinking on export promotion strategies from several aspects—policy, structure, markets from the government, business and academic points of view and hence this study is unique in certain respects.

The major constraints in export study in India are the low priority given to research as against marketing, a greater dependence on desk research, long time gap in research findings reaching the practitioners, multiplicity of organisations sponsoring research, less attention to policy research, limited research on invisible exports and concentration of research on immediate issues.

Despite the large number of institutions, (100 Universities, IIFT, NCAER, Institutes of Management, twenty Export Promotion Councils, nine Commodity Boards, four ED Authorities, one dozen premier Chambers of Commerce) research output has been very low. Lack of funds especially foreign exchange has been a major impediment despite the Market Development Fund established by the Government of India. Research further suffers from lack of specialised manpower, limited facilities at the Universities, indifferent attitudes of users (business carry on ad hoc export strategies rather than research based).

There is an established need for integration for export research organisations as in Hong Kong, Singapore and Korea, jointly supported and funded by business, government and academia. A central data bank on export would meet the needs of different organisations.

1.3 IMPORTANCE OF THE STUDY

The present study is expected to be of very great significance to a number of persons and organisations. The study shall provide an in depth background analysis and interpretation which will help the teaching and researching communities in their academic pursuits. It would help government officers and political leaders in formulating future export promotion strategies. The findings would indeed be of great practical significance to exporters of India in as much as they could use them for their deliberations with the government. The frank and independent analysis of the malpractice resorted to by Indian exporters would encourage self critical thinking by Indian exporters and adopting the right export ethics, both in their own long term interests as well as that of the nation. The study could also be profitable to importers in other countries as it would provide a clearer picture of India's export promotion—the strategies, policies, schemes, incentives and measures.

1.4 OBJECTIVES OF THE STUDY

The present research has been undertaken with the following objectives in view to acquire a sound knowledge of economic theory, trade theory, international finance and related fields

- Recapitulate development of India's foreign trade in the past and how they influence the present.

- To identify the currently significant barriers to export including the obstructing or accelerating role being played the various regional economic blocks.
- To acquire familiarity with export promotion endeavours being made in developed countries like Canada, UK, Italy, West Germany and France and in countries of Asia like Japan, South Korea, Singapore, China (PRC), Hong Kong, Thailand, Malaysia, Indonesia and Pakistan.
- To bring under sharp focus and critical analysis, the export promotion policies, strategies, etc. formulated and implemented so far in India.
- To project how liberalisation of the Indian economy could be more effectively utilised to promote Indian exports.
- To formulate some suggestions at the micro level for making export promotion more effective in the future.
- To develop a future model of export promotion strategies in India.

1.5 SCOPE OF THE STUDY

Though this study relates to foreign trade of India, instead of repeating in detail the development and growth of India's foreign trade in terms of value, volume, direction, composition and terms of trade, attention has been focused chiefly on the export promotion strategies, policies, schemes, incentives, measures, etc. The purpose behind this rather unique approach has been to focus sharply on the problems under research so as to make the analysis, findings and conclusions really meaningful for all the parties considered. By and large, the research has been concentrated on development in the field of export promotion during the last fifteen years. The researcher being based in Hong Kong has easy and convenient access to quantitative data and qualitative information from the South East Asian countries, which are also developing very fast under the impact of export promotion. Hence particular attention was paid to transplanting export promotion strategies from South East Asian countries into India.

1.6 DATA COLLECTION

For a study like the present one, it was thought necessary to collect, analyse and interpret quantitative data and qualitative information from a large number of sources. Data and information was sourced from India, Hong Kong and several other South East Asian countries. The researcher has freely made use of the secondary data contained in the various publications and studies of concerned institutions in India and in South East Asia. Further, information from the publications of international and multinational agencies have been freely used. A former exporter himself, this researcher had the privilege and the pleasure of holding personal interviews with a large number of exporters, government officers and senior members of the academic profession in India, South East Asia and the United States. An effort has been made to submit in this present study, only those recommendations and suggestions whose feasibility has already been discussed with the various parties concerned, involved in the export trade.

Reliance was placed on published materials available both in India and elsewhere- (Hong Kong), Government and Central Bank Publications in addition to publications from Exim Bank , Commercial Banks, Export Promotion Councils. Seminar proceedings from FICCI (Federation of Indian Chambers of Commerce and Industry) Assocham (Associated Chambers of Commerce, Indian

Council of Economic ICRIER Research were indeed helpful. Personnel interviews and discussions were held with Government bodies like the Planning Commission, India Investment Centre and private institutions like CMIE.

Detailed discussions were also held with academics of the Indian Institute of Foreign Trade, the several IIMs, Jawaharlal Nehru University as well as the Delhi School of Economics. Data and reports of World Bank, IMF, ADB and OECD were made use of.

Interpretation of the data and conclusions are entirely the researcher's and deficiencies or errors, if any, are entirely the author's.

1.7 LIMITATIONS OF THE STUDY

Any study on foreign trade and particularly on export promotion is, by its very nature, fascinating. Though one would like to examine a number of aspects, one has severe limitations to work under. That differentiates a study by an individual from that of an institution. The researcher had to work under severe constraints and limitations of time and hence the study of export promotion around the world had to be confined to only a few countries. Also the researcher could not personally interview as many importers of goods from India, abroad as desired. The liberalisation process set in motion in 1991, has been inconsistently pursued. So it shall not be possible to examine the exact impact of liberalisation on export promotion. Lastly, the researcher could not discuss at length, the future models of export promotion strategies in India with many Indian exporters, Indian policy makers and importers of Indian products abroad. Perhaps, this is one area which calls for continuous future research.

CHAPTER 2

HISTORICAL BACKGROUND

2.1 EXPORTS IN ANTIQUITY

India's foreign trade can be traced as far back as the Rig Vedic period (1200 B.C). Ancient literature refers to a thriving sea-borne trade with China (Kosakaras), Java (Yavan Dwipa), Sumatra (Swaran Dwipa), Red Sea (Lohita Sagar), Babylon, Assyria, Elam, Judala, Egypt, Arabia, Persia, Burma, Ceylon, Japan and Greece. During that era, cotton manufactures were the principal exports followed by dye stuffs (indigo being a monopoly), silk and muslin, spices, cutlery, metal wares, sugar, perfumes and cosmetics, sandalwood and teak, ivory work, animal and animal skins. Chief articles of import included bullion, precious stones, woollen goods, wines, horses and minerals. India's geographical position, midway between east and west served as a link between east and west and part of her exports were in the nature of entreport trade. In contrast to the present times, export mostly consisted of manufactured goods and India enjoyed a favourable balance of trade. (*Source* : Varshney Roshanlal, 1954)

2.2 MUSLIM AND MOGHUL PERIOD

Following the attacks of Mohammed Ghazni in 712 AD, India was the hunting ground for several attacking forces from the North West disrupting trade, though trade in the west coast flourished. According to Marco Polo who visited India between 1271 and 1294 AD, the country continued as one of the chief markets of Asia. The Moghul empire established by Babur (1526 AD), encouraged trade with the Dutch, Portuguese and British.

The activities of foreigners helped widen the market for Indian products though the share of trade was curtailed. The composition of exports continued to be the same as before and total exports of the country during the sixteenth century has been estimated to be around 85,000 tons (by Dr. Balakrishna) and valued at Rs. 100 crores (by Prof. K.T. Shah). There was no attempt to protect indeginous industries and tariff was for revenue purposes alone and import of precious metals attracted low duties.

2.3 THE EUROPEAN PERIOD

Among the Europeans, the British gained concessions from the Moghul emperors and slowly began penetrating into Indian politics and, especially after the Battle of Plassey (1757 AD), established themselves in Bengal. This helped the development of African, American and Continental markets and enhanced the monopoly of the East India Company. With the Industrial revolution in England, export of manufactured items, especially textiles was discouraged while export of raw materials and food grains received a boost.

Since 1870, foreign trade activated and moulded India's economy, as evidenced from phenomenal development of agriculture and cash crops. While commercial contact with the west helped lay foundations for the railways, industries, medical facilities and other amenities, it was UK which benefited most from India's foreign trade as almost all plantations, modern industries and auxiliary services were owned by the British.

Economic progress and continuous increase in both import and export was evident till around 1913-14. Food stuffs, tea, coffee, raw cotton, raw jute, oil seeds and hides and skins made up the exports and the imports consisted of sugar, textiles and machinery. Trade with non-empire countries like USA, the Continent, Japan and Far East improved while trade with UK declined.

2.4 EXPORTS DURING THE FIRST WORLD WAR PERIOD

The first World War period (1914-18) saw India lose the position it had gained earlier. The terms of trade became unfavourable, imports declined and the nation was deprived of prime necessities although it enjoyed an export surplus. The factors which affected India's foreign trade included cessation of trade with enemy countries, impoverishment of many economies due to war, scarcity of tonnage (due to withdrawal of UK and enemy ships for war) as well as currency and exchange difficulties. The direction of India's exports veered towards UK and British empire.

In the post war period, India's exports improved till the depression of 1929 which saw widespread disequilibrium in world trade and resultant contraction in volume. Economic nationalism gained a stranglehold and free trade gave place to regional economic units—the "Gold Block" and the "Sterling Block". The inter-war period witnessed a change in the composition of India's foreign trade due to increased domestic production capabilities.

Exports of manufactured goods (jute goods, oilseed products, tanned skins and semi-processed raw materials) increased while capital goods and industrial raw materials grew in their proportion in imports.

2.5 EXPORT DURING SECOND WORLD WAR PERIOD

With the outbreak of the Second World War in 1939, belligerency was thrust on India. Her economy had to be adapted to war efforts of UK and be a major source of supply of men and materials. International trade was distorted by military movements, availability of trade routes and shipping tonnage, diversion of economic resources to war, blockades and supply of foreign exchange. With the entry of Japan in the war and spread of fighting to Middle East and North Africa, India's strategic position became more important and her exports, imports and re-exports saw growth resulting in favourable balance of trade (454% over pre-war level).

2.6 POST WAR PERIOD

Under the Defence of India Ordinance 1944, the government imposed many restrictions on foreign exchange and export. The Exchange control was intended to conserve foreign exchange by limiting remittances except for essential purposes. Export control took the form of prohibition of exports to enemy countries, trading with black listed companies in neutral countries, and exports of certain products without licence and export to specific countries only under open general licence. A natural sequel to the policy of conservation of foreign exchange was the imposition of import control.

The controls on imports and exports had the effect of drastically bringing down foreign trade on private account and diverting the same to the supply department of the government of India. The United Kingdom Commercial Corporation (UKCC) set-up in April, 1940 acquired extensive monopoly rights in foreign trade, to the detriment of Indian exporters. However the war had catalysed rapid industrialisation of the country and consequent reduction in imports. But with the half-hearted sympathy of the government, India missed the opportunity to establish many heavy industries by importing capital machinery. Though India did not lack the money or the material resources, the only industry established in the country was the iron and steel industry.

Immediately after the war, many authors in addition to the government of India hailed India's emergence as a creditor nation from a debtor nation. However, on close scrutiny, this status referred only to the field of governmental indebtedness.

2.7 POST INDEPENDENCE PERIOD

In the wake of Independence in 1947 and partition of the sub-continent, disequilibrium of the economy set in. Size of foreign trade increased since what was formerly domestic trade had to be considered foreign trade. Raw material, like jute, cotton and food grain supplies were reduced and an adverse balance of trade with Pakistan resulted. Overall, there was a fall in exports primarily due to physical shortages in certain raw materials and an increase in consumption which led to removal of export duties. Heavy imports of food, capital goods and other essential goods resulted in an adverse balance of trade. The import policy was linked to the foreign exchange position and hence subject to periodic revisions.

Distortion caused by the war years in the direction of foreign trade was corrected, as India resumed trade with erstwhile enemy countries. The direction of both imports and export were influenced by currency considerations. Share of UK in exports was considerably lowered, at the same time USA's importance grew.

The composition of India's exports also underwent changes. While proportion of food, drink and tobacco to total exports remained static, manufactured goods recorded an increase in jute manufacture, while cotton manufactures and processed hides and skins declined.

To sum up, the larger effect of the war, independence and subsequent partition has been:

- Export surplus in some food grains and pulses disappear.

- Export surplus of raw jute, raw cotton and raw hides and skins was severely curtailed.
- Exports of cotton manufactures and jute manufactures increased, though dependent on availability of foreign raw materials.
- Tea exports increased, despite greater consumption mainly because of increased production.

2.8 STERLING BALANCES

During the Second World War, exports as well as foreign exchange was strictly controlled and from 1940, only Sterling and Dollar remained approved currencies. India was able to repatriate the entire amount of her external debt of £ 360 million as a result of Sterling balances accumulated to the credit of Reserve Bank of India. Sir Jeremy Raisnan in his 1943-44 budget speech observed "India has completed the transition from a debtor to a creditor country." Sterling assets were estimated at £ 1300 million. At the outset, independent India began with a comfortable balance of payment position.

2.9 EXPORTS UNDER THE FIVE YEAR PLANS

The external sector of the economy received but limited attention till about the Third Plan period as India had no serious foreign problem since the Second World War and a deliberately formulated Export promotion strategy was not considered a necessary part of the development effort.

The constitution of the Import and Export Committee in 1962, was the first serious attempt at developing a policy on Import and Export. The Committee noted that both central and state governments were not alive to the primacy of export promotion "Only as late as 1970 did Government of India formulate an Export Policy on promoting exports.

The average level of exports during the first plan period (1951-1956) was Rs. 605 crores, with a deficit of Rs. 130 crores, except for 1951-52, which recorded a high of Rs. 716 crores, due to the Korean war.

The Second Plan period (1956-61) witnessed substantial growth in imports averaging Rs. 973 crores per annum, while exports remained at Rs. 606 crores/annum, increasing the deficit to Rs. 367 crores.

The Third Plan period (1961-66) saw average exports rise to Rs. 753 crores, due to the introduction of export incentives, establishment of export service institutions and attempt to improve export infrastructure. However the increase in imports raised the deficit to Rs. 487 crores.

During the next three years (1966-1968) following the devaluation of the Rupee, exports jumped to Rs. 1157 crores, but with a corresponding increase in the deficit to Rs. 760 crores per annum.

An 'Export or Perish' period during the Fourth plan saw the Parliament pass the Export Policy Resolution in 1970. The trade deficit declined drastically to an average of Rs. 163 crores per annum. In 1972-73 , for the first time in many years, a surplus on trade account was recorded.

The oil crisis of 1973 led to a sudden and substantial jump in the import bill and the trade deficit reverted to Rs. 432 crores in 1973-74.

Philosophies of 'Export or Perish' and 'Import Substitution' and 'Export Promotion' yielded place to a philosophy of 'export more and import more' during the Fifth Plan period (1974-79), which saw substantial growth in both exports and imports, though it lead to an increase of trade deficit to Rs. 810 crores per annum.

The subsequent two plan periods (1980-85) and (1985-90) were.periods of steady growth in exports, imports and trade deficit. It is noteworthy that while average annual level of exports grew slightly more than three and half times between the Fifth Plan and Seventh Plan, imports grew more than four and half times leading to substantial growth in the negative trade balance from Rs. 810 crores in 1974-79 to Rs. 7743 crores per annum during the Seventh Plan period.

The subsequent three years (1991-94) witnessed historic changes in foreign trade policy, the main thrust of which was all round economic liberalisation. The Government initiated steps which were directed towards dismantling the complex system of export incentives and shifting emphasis from government regulations to market forces. As part of the exercise, the Rupee was made convertible on the trade account. Both exports and imports recorded growth and the trade deficit increased to Rs. 9697 crore. The provisional estimate of Foreign trade in 1995-96 was exports Rs. 106,353 crore and imports Rs. 122,678 crore, leaving a negative trade balance of Rs. 16,325 crore. Table 2.2 shows that in 97-98, exports-stood at Rs. 126,286 crore, imports at Rs. 151,554 crore and negatives balance at Rs. 25,268 crores.

2.10 COMPOSITION OF INDIA'S EXPORTS

The table 2.3 details composition of India's Exports by major commodities. Gems and jewellery have emerged in, recent years, as the single largest group, followed by clothing (garments) and engineering goods, whereas during the sixties it were jute manufactures, tea and iron ore that dominated. Another new addition, though limited in value, is software. To sum up, the more dynamic growth sectors appear to be cotton piece goods, leather manufactures, marine products, oil cakes, chemicals, handicrafts, clothing, engineering goods and gems and jewellery.

A closer look would indicate that the items which dominate the Indian export scene can be broadly classified into three.

(1) Products in which India enjoys comparative advantage due to climate, topography, resource endowment. This would include items like tea, jute, jute manufactures, tobacco, spices, coffee, iron ore, marine products, oil cakes and leather.

(2) Items involving low technology, and labour skills and intensity, such as cotton textiles, cashews, chemicals, engineering goods, handicrafts and clothing.

(3) Items which are mainly dependent on imports and labour skills available. These include gems and jewellery (especially diamonds) and cashewnuts.

In addition to products above, other main items that are exported include processed foods, silk goods, rice, synthetic textiles and petroleum products, which are non-traditional items. Traditional items like tea, textiles, jute and jute products constituted main components of the export basket in earlier years, whereas now, particularly since 1990's, non-traditional items dominate India's exports.

The latest data for the year 1997-98 indicate that the manufactured goods, which have emerged as potential export items after industrialisation in recent years, account for 74.8% of total exports .

SHARE OF INDIVIDUAL ITEMS IN TOTAL EXPORTS (%)

Product Groups	*1996-97*	*1997-98*
Gems & Jewellery	14.20	15.06
Textiles, yarn & made ups	12.12	12.57
Ready made garments	11.21	11.11
Leather & leather mfrs.	4.80	4.33
Drugs, pharmaceuticals, fine chemicals	3.65	4.14
Marine products	3.37	3.42
Agricultural & allied products	20.50	18.84

Of late software is emerging as a very big and promising item in India's export basket and foreign exchange earnings from exports of computer software and services grew from Rs. 4113 crore in 1996-97 to Rs. 6800 crore in 1997-98, registering an increase of 65.33% over the previous year.

2.11 DIRECTION OF INDIA'S EXPORTS

The major markets for India's export products region wise have been the European Union, North America and Asia (ESCAP region), which accounted for nearly 75% of India's total exports during 1992-93 (The share of Africa, Eastern Europe and South America total just over 9%).

The largest market is provided by the European Union (notably UK and Germany) while USA is the single largest buyer of Indian products. Within the Asian region, Japan, Hong Kong and Singapore are the major buyers. India's exports to East European countries including the former USSR have undergone a metamorphosis in recent times. This was the region that consequent to the trade and payments arrangements, accounted for maximum growth in Indian exports, till the beginning of the 90's. From less than Rs. 10 crore per annum during the first plan period, India's exports to USSR and East Europe grew to more than Rs. 8514 crore in 90-91. Subsequently, due to economic restructuring in these countries and due to the discontinuance of the trade and payments arrangements, India's exports started declining to Rs. 4624 crore in 93-94 and Rs. 3048 crore during April-Feb. 1998.

The share of Asia including the Middle East continued to grow from 14.3% in 1990-91 to 22.7% in 1996-97, which trend has continued into 1997-98. However the share of exports to Japan showed a decline from 9.3% in 1990-91 to 6% in 1996-97. With such an uneven pattern in the direction of exports, India has to diversify its markets while intensifying its efforts in existing markets.

Table 2.1

India's Foreign Trade
Exports, Imports & Trade Balance and Share in World Exports

	US $ million			*Change over previous year (%)*		*India's exports as % of*
	Exports	*Imports*	*Trade balance*	*Exports*	*Imports*	*World exports*
1950-51	1,269.00	1,273.00	-4.00			2.05
1960-61	1,346.00	2,353.00	-1,007.00	0.22	16.72	1.04
1970-71	2,031.00	2,162.00	-131.00	8.84	3.49	0.64
1980-81	8,486.00	15,869.00	-7,383.00	6.78	40.17	0.42
1990-91	18,143.00	24,075.00	-5,932.00	9.22	13.46	0.53
1991-92	17,865.00	19,411.00	-1,546.00	-1.53	-19.37	0.51
1992-93	18,537.00	21,882.00	-3,345.00	3.76	12.73	0.51
1993-94	22,238.00	23,306.00	-1,068.00	19.97	6.51	0.61
1994-95	26,330.00	28,654.00	-2,324.00	18.40	22.95	0.64
1995-96	31,830.00	36,369.00	-4,539.00	21.38	28.74	0.60
1996-97	33,106.00	38,548.00	-5,442.00	4.01	5.99	0.60
1997-98	33,980.00	40,779.00	-6,799.00	2.64	5.79	NA

Source : Annual Reports of Ministry of Commerce, Govt. of India.

Table 2.2

India's Foreign Trade During Five Year Plans

(Value : Rs. Crore)

	Import	*Export*	*Balance of Trade*
Annual Average of First Plan (1951-56)	1,052	926	-126
Annual Average of Second Plan (1956-61)	1,553	978	-575
Annual Average of Third Plan (1966-69)	1,950	1,178	-772
Annual Average of Annual Plan Periods (1966-69)	1,991	1,247	-744
Annual Average of Fourth Plan (1969-74)	1,972	1,807	-165
Annual Average of Fifth Plan (1974-78)	5,147	4,441	-706
Average of two rolling plans (1978-80)	7,977	6,072	-1,905
Annual Average of Sixth Plan (1980-85)	14,673	8,955	-5,718
Average of Seventh Plan (1985-90)	25,130	17,387	-7,743
Average of Eighth Plan (Annual 1990-95)	63,186	56,398	-6,788
1995-96	122,678	106,353	-16,325
1996-97	136,844	117,525	-19,319
1997-98	151,554	126,286	-25,268

Source : Annual Report of Ministry of Commerce & DGCIS, Calcutta.

Note : Previous values in post devaluation (1966) terms adjusted.

Chart 2.3

Composition of Exports & Imports

(Percent)

1996-1997

Exports

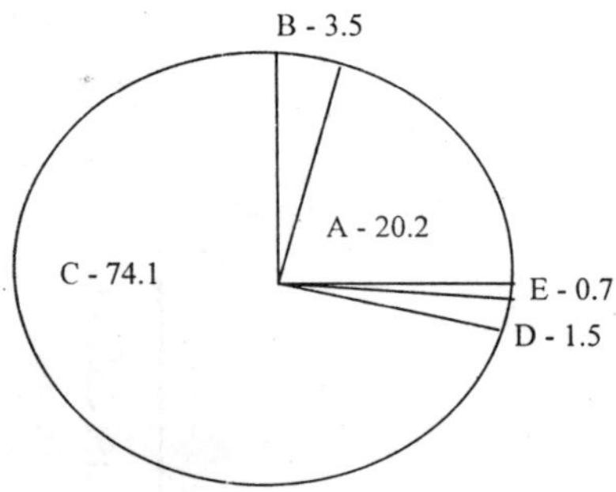

A - Agriculture and Allied Products
B - Ores and Minerals
C - Manufactured Goods
D - Crude and Petroleum Products
E - Others

US$33,106.1 Million

Imports

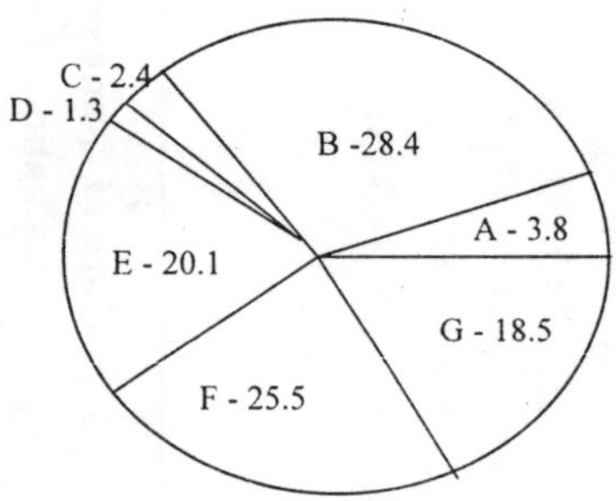

A - Food and Allied Products
B - Fuel
C - Fertilisrs
D - Paper Board Manuf. and News Print
E - Capital Goods
F - Other Bulk Items
G - Others

US$38,548.2 Million

Source : Economic Survey (1997-98), Ministry of Finance, Government of India.

Chart 2.4

Direction of India's Trade

(Percent)

1996-1997

Destination of Exports

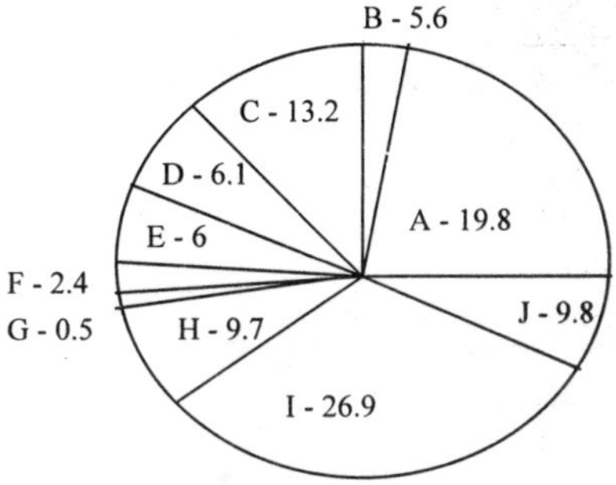

US$33,106.1 Million

Sources of Imports

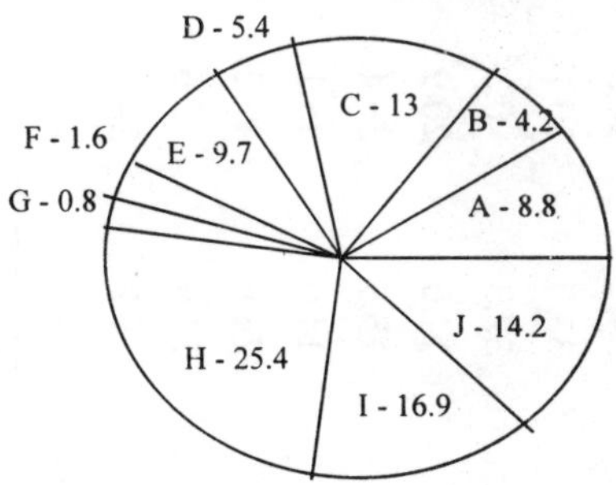

US$38,548.2 Million

A - U.S.A.
B - Germany
C - Other E. U.
D - U. K.
E - Japan
F - Russia
G - Other East Europe
H - OPEC
I - L. D. C.s
J - Others

Source : Economic Survey (1997-98), Ministry of Finance, Government of India.

Table 2.5

Region-Wise Exports : 1993-94—1996-97

REGION	*Growth Rate in Exports* 93-94	94-95	95-96	96-97	*% Share in India's Total Exports* 93-94	94-95	95-96	96-97
WEST EUROPE	9.8	20.9	19.2	-1.2	28.9	29.5	29.1	27.6
(a) ECM Countries	10.5	21.3	19.7	-1.8	26.1	26.7	26.5	25.0
(b) EFTA Countries	6.9	22.2	5.9	3.4	2.2	2.3	2.0	2.0
ASIA & OCEANA	34.2	14.5	23.3	4.3	41.0	39.6	40.4	40.5
(a) ESCAP	33.0	20.1	26.1	2.2	29.4	29.8	31.1	30.6
(b) Others	37.3	0.3	14.7	11.2	11.6	9.8	9.3	10.0
AFRICA	14.0	20.9	68.9	-4.8	3.7	3.8	5.3	4.8
AMERICA	15.5	26.4	9.7	19.1	20.1	21.5	19.5	22.3
(a) North	14.0	25.1	10.2	18.3	19.0	20.1	18.3	20.8
(b) South	74.8	49.2	14.3	37.7	0.7	0.8	0.8	1.0
EAST EUROPE	22.9	5.6	26.8	-20.2	4.5	4.0	4.2	3.2
CIS	6.9	24.3	29.5	-25.5	2.9	3.1	3.3	2.4
REST OF CIS COUNTRIES	-	-77.5	188.2	6.2	0.6	0.1	0.3	0.3
TOTAL	20.0	18.4	20.8	4.1	100.0	100.0	100.0	100.0

Table 2.6

Leading Exporters and Importers in World Merchandise Trade, 1997

(Billion dollars and percentage)

Rank	*Exporters*	*Value*	*Share*	*Annual percentage change*	*Rank*	*Importers*	*Value*	*Share*	*Annual percentage change*
1	2	3	4	5	6	7	8	9	10
1	United States	688.7	12.6	10	1	United States	899.0	16.0	9
2	Germany	511.7	9.4	-2	2	Germany	441.5	7.8	-4
3	Japan	421.0	7.7	2	3	Japan	338.8	6.0	-3
4	France	289.5	5.3	0	4	United Kingdom	308.2	5.5	7
5	United Kingdom	281.6	5.2	8	5	France	268.4	4.8	-5
6	Italy	238.2	4.4	-5	6	Hong Kong, China	213.3	3.8	6
7	Canada	214.4	3.9	6		retained imports a	52.4	0.9	10
8	Netherlands	193.8	3.5	-5	7	Italy	208.1	3.7	0
9	Hong Kong, China	188.2	3.4	4	8	Canada	200.9	3.6	15
	domestic exports	27.3	0.5	0	9	Netherland	177.2	3.1	-4
	re-exports	160.9	2.9	5	10	Belgium-Luxembourg	155.8	2.8	-3
10	China	182.7	3.3	21					
11	Belgium-Luxembourg	168.2	3.1	-1	11	Korea, Rep. of	144.6	2.6	-4

(Contd.)

(Contd.)

1	2	3	4	5	6	7	8	9	10
12	Korea, Rep. of	136.2	2.5	5	12	China	142.4	2.5	3
13	Singapore	125.0	2.3	0	13	Singapore	132.4	2.4	1
	domestic exports	72.4	1.3	-1		retained imports a	79.9	1.4	0
	re-exports	52.6	1.0	2	14	Spain	122.7	2.2	1
14	Taipei, Chinese	121.9	2.2	5	15	Mexico	113.3	2.0	24
15	Mexico	110.4	2.0	15	16	Taipei, Chinese	113.2	2.0	12
16	Spain	104.3	1.9	2	17	Malaysia	79.0	1.4	1
17	Sweden	82.7	1.5	-3	18	Switzerland	76.0	1.3	-4
18	Malaysia	78.4	1.4	1	19	Australia	65.9	1.2	1
19	Switzerland	76.2	1.4	-6	20	Sweden	65.4	1.2	-2
20	Russian Fed. b	66.3	1.2	-4					
21	Australia	62.9	1.2	4	21	Brazil	65.0	1.2	14
22	Austria	58.6	1.1	1	22	Austria	64.8	1.2	-4
23	Thailand	57.4	1.1	3	23	Thailand	63.6	1.1	-13
24	Indonesia	53.5	1.0	7	24	Russian Feb. b	48.8	0.9	13
25	Ireland	53.1	1.0	9	25	Turkey	48.6	0.9	13
26	Brazil	53.0	1.0	11	26	Denmark	44.6	0.8	-1
27	Saudi Aribia c	52.8	1.0	-7	27	Poland	42.3	0.8	14
28	Denmark	48.9	0.9	-4	28	Indonesia	42.0	0.7	-2

(Contd.)

(Contd.)

1	2	3	4	5	6	7	8	9	10
29	Norway	47.7	0.9	-2	29	India	40.4	0.7	8
30	Finland	40.8	0.7	1	30	Ireland	39.2	0.7	9
31	India	33.9	0.6	3	31	Philippines	38.0	0.7	11
32	South Africa d	30.3	0.6	6	32	Norway	35.5	0.6	0
33	Turkey	26.2	0.5	14	33	Portugal	33.6	0.6	-5
34	Poland	25.8	0.5	5	34	South Africa d	32.9	0.6	9
35	Argentina	25.5	0.5	7	35	Israel	30.8	0.5	-3
36	Philippines	25.3	0.5	24	36	Finland	30.7	0.5	0
37	United Arab Emirates c	25.0	0.5	-4	37	Argentina	30.3	0.5	28
38	Portugal	23.2	0.4	-6	38	United Arab Emirates c	27.8	0.5	7
39	Venezuela	23.1	0.4	0	39	Saudi Arabia	27.3	0.5	-2
40	Czech Rep.	22.8	0.4	4	40	Czech Rep. e	27.2	0.5	-2
41	Israel	22.5	0.4	9	41	Greece	25.2	0.4	17
42	Hungary	19.1	0.3	22	42	Hungary	21.2	0.4	17
43	Iran, Islamic Rep. of c	17.7	0.3	-6	43	Chile	19.9	0.4	11
44	Chile	16.9	0.3	10	44	Colombia	15.4	0.3	12
45	Kuwait	14.8	0.3	0	45	New Zealand	14.5	0.3	-1
46	Nigeria c	14.5	0.3	1	46	Iran, Islamic Rep. of c	13.8	0.2	7
47	New Zealand	14.1	0.3	-3	47	Egypt	13.2	0.2	1

(Contd.)

(Contd.)

1	2	3	4	5	6	7	8	9	10
48	Algeria c	12.7	0.2	10	48	Pakistan	11.6	0.2	-4
49	Colombia	11.5	0.2	9	49	Venezuela c	11.5	0.2	16
50	Greece	10.8	0.2	-9	50	Viet Nam c	11.3	0.2	1
	Total of above f	5223.7	95.6	-		Total of above f	5237.0	93.0	-
	World f	5460.0	100.0	3		World f	5630.0	100.0	3

a Retained imports are defined as imports less re-exports. See the Technical Notes.

b Excludes trade with the Baltic States and the CIS Including trade with these States would lift Russian exports and imports to $87 billion and $68 billion respectively.

c Secretariat estimates.

d Throughout this report the merchandise figures refer to the Customs Union of Southern Africa.

e Imports are valued f.o.b.

f Includes significant re-exports or import for re-export.

Note : *For annual data 1987-97, see Appendix Tables A3 and A4.*

Source : WTO.

Table 2.7

Leading Exporters and Importers in World Trade in Commercial Services, 1997

(Billion dollars and percentage)

Rank	Exporters	Value	Share	Annual percentage change	Rank	Importers	Value	Share	Annual percentage change
1	2	3	4	5	6	7	8	9	10
1	United States	229.9	17.5	7	1	United States	150.1	11.6	7
2	United Kingdom	85.5	6.5	12	2	Japan	122.1	9.4	-5
3	France	80.3	6.1	-3	3	Germany	120.1	9.3	-5
4	Germany	75.4	5.7	-4	4	Italy	70.1	5.4	5
5	Italy	71.7	5.5	4	5	United Kingdom	68.6	5.3	9
6	Japan	68.1	5.2	3	6	France	62.1	4.8	-5
7	Netherland	48.5	3.7	-1	7	Netherland	43.8	3.4	-2
8	Spain	43.6	3.3	-1	8	Canada	35.9	2.8	1
9	Hong Kong, China	37.3	2.8	0	9	Belgium-Luxembourg	32.1	2.5	-3
10	Belgium-Luxembourg	34.0	2.6	-2	10	China	30.1	2.3	34
11	Singapore	30.4	2.3	2	11	Korea, Rep. of	29.0	2.2	0
12	Canada	29.3	2.2	2	12	Austria	27.4	2.1	-10
13	Austria a	28.5	2.2	...	13	Spain	24.3	1.9	1
14	Switzerland	25.6	2.0	-2	14	Taipei, Chinese	24.1	1.9	2

(Contd.)

(Contd.)

1	2	3	4	5	6	7	8	9	10
15	Korea, Rep. of	25.4	1.9	12	15	Hong Kong, China	22.7	1.8	6
16	China	24.5	1.9	19	16	Sweden	19.5	1.5	4
17	Turkey	19.2	1.5	49	17	Singapore	19.4	1.5	1
18	Australia	18.2	1.4	1	18	Brazil	19.0	1.5	36
19	Sweden	17.6	1.3	5	19	Russian Fed.	18.7	1.4	0
20	Taipei, Chinese	17.0	1.3	5	20	Australia	18.2	1.4	0
21	Denmark b	16.5	1.3	...	21	Thailand	17.2	1.3	-11
22	Thailand	15.8	1.2	-5	22	Malaysia	16.8	1.3	0
23	Philippines	15.1	1.2	17	23	Indonesia	16.1	1.2	9
24	Malaysia	14.5	1.1	4	24	Ireland	15.0	1.2	12
25	Norway	14.3	1.1	2	25	Denmark b	14.7	1.1	...
26	Russian Fed.	13.5	1.0	4	26	Norway	14.5	1.1	8
27	Mexico	11.2	0.9	5	27	Switzerland	14.1	1.1	-8
28	Poland b	10.1	0.8	...	28	Philippines	14.1	1.1	50
29	Egypt	9.7	0.7	6	29	Saudi Arabia	13.9	1.1	11
30	Greece b	9.4	0.7	...	30	Mexico	11.5	0.9	16
31	India b	8.8	0.7	...	31	India b	11.0	0.9	...
32	Israel	8.3	0.6	5	32	Israel	10.9	0.8	5
33	Brazil	7.9	0.6	37	33	Turkey	8.1	0.6	34
34	Portugal	7.5	0.6	-8	34	Finland	8.1	0.6	-6

(Contd.)

(Contd.)

1	2	3	4	5	6	7	8	9	10
35	Czech Rep.	7.0	0.5	-13	35	Egypt	7.2	0.6	52
36	Finland	6.8	0.5	5	36	Poland b	6.5	0.5	...
37	Indonesia	6.8	0.5	5	37	Portugal	6.1	0.5	-6
38	Ireland	6.0	0.5	8	38	South Africa	6.0	0.5	4
39	Ukraine	4.9	0.4	3	39	Argentina	6.0	0.5	12
40	South Africa	4.9	0.4	11	40	Czech Rep.	5.3	0.4	-14
	Total of above	1204.2	91.8	3		Total of above	1175.2	90.7	2
	World	1310.0	100.0	3		World	1295.0	100.0	2

a Growth rate in 1997 is affected by changes in the methodological treatment of unallocated flows.

b Secretariat estimates.

Note : Figures for a number of countries and territories have been estimated by the Secretariat. Annual percentage changes and rankings are affected by continuity breaks in the series for a large number of economies, and by limitations in cross-country comparability. See the Technical Note. Annual statistics 1987-97 are given in Appendix Tables A5 and A6.

Source : WTO.

Chapter 3

Barriers to Export and Economic Integration Around the World

3.1 INTRODUCTION

An interesting development in international economy during the post World War II period has been the setting up of the four international financial institutions namely International Monetary Fund (IMF), International Bank for Reconstruction and Development (IBRD), International Development Association (IDA) and the International Finance Corporation (IFC) to facilitate the free flow of international investment and trade. However, during this period, a number of barriers to exports have emerged in the shape of Protectionism, multi-fibre arrangement (MFA), anti-dumping measures, non-tariff barriers, new international regulations based on human rights and ecological considerations. As if this was not enough to make the tasks of the international agencies more difficult, a number of major trading blocs have since been created around the world like NAFTA, EU, SAPTA, ASEAN and APEC which have rather restricted the free flow of international investment and trade. It is rather paradoxical to see two opposite trends emerging on the horizon of world trade. On the one hand, international trade is moving towards freer trade through globalisation, though trading blocks seem to encourage regional trade.

This chapter, deals first with barriers to Indian exports at the macro and the micro levels, followed by a brief overview of the emergence of World Trade Organisation, South Asian Preferential Trade Agreement, Association of South East Asian Nations, Asia Pacific Economic Co-operation, North American Free Trade Agreement and the European Union which may have possibilities of restricting or accelerating India's exports.

3.2 TRADE BARRIERS AT THE MACRO LEVEL

Despite professions of free trade, most countries erect barriers to international flows of goods and services. The developing countries have to face many tariff and non-tariff barriers like :

1. Price based constraints (tariffs and subsidies)
2. Quantity limits (quotas, embargoes)
3. Buyers or Sellers cartels (OPEC, Commodity Agreements, MFA)
4. Financial limits (exchange controls, etc.)
5. Standards, testing, labelling and certification (sometimes regional standards)
6. Import licensing (restrictive licensing practices)
7. Government procurement (buy national policies)
8. Lack of intellectual property protection
9. Service barriers (insistence on imports being carried by national vessels)

Tariffs are charged mostly on an *ad valorem* basis on imports. The US tariff rate ranges from 0-117%, making domestic products more competitive. Subsidies to local production are also intended to improve, competitiveness of domestic industries. Under the new WTO regulations, subsidies are likely to meet with objections.

Quotas, which are quantity limitations on international trade, are sometimes imposed under the guise of 'voluntary export restraints'. The Multifibre Arrangement (MFA), which is to be abolished by the year 2005, would help the garment and textile exports of many a developing country. Most embargoes are placed on imports for clearly political reasons. Both quotas and embargoes limit access by consumers to better priced imports.

The non-tariff barriers (NTBs) range from bureaucratic delays in processing import permits, to quality standards that preclude foreign goods and to 'buy national programs'. NTBs raise the cost of imports as well as lowers availability of imported products. Other NTBs in evidence around the world include regulations on labelling, health and safety standards.

Indian exports are subject to many barriers in her major markets. USA had aimed anti-dumping and countervailing duties on steel items along with wire rods and sulfanilic acid. Anti-dumping investigations have to conform to WTO regime but cost of defending tends to be prohibitive. India has also been under 'watch list' of section 301 (special 301 and super 301) of the US Tariff Act which is considered highly discriminatory.

The NTBs faced in the Japanese market are the slow import clearances due to lengthy customs procedures, phytosanitary, packaging, environmental and health standards affecting food items, while agricultural exports face procedural problems.

As regards tariffs, it is observed that during the eight rounds of negotiations under the General Agreement on Tariffs and Trade held since 1947, developed countries have brought down their average level of tariffs from more than 40% to a post Uruguay level of 3.9% as indicated below:

	Average Tariffs %	
	Pre-UR	*Post UR*
EU	5.7	3.6
USA	5.4	3.9
Japan	1.9	1.7

Source : IMF International Trade Policy,
The Uruguay Round and Beyond 1994.

The NTBs in Germany include ban on import/use of products using Benzedrine based dyes and azo-dyes. Germans insist on eco- friendly packaging and there are fixed standards on chemical residues on products such as tea. Indian seafood exporters have been facing stringent health regulations in the Italian market which lead to delays at ports. In Netherlands, public opinion is strongly against the use of child labour in the carpet industry in India. In France, strict technical/security standards are applied to import of bicycles as well as pharmaceutical products.

Hong Kong is a free port and has no significant NTBs and no specific anti-dumping measures against Indian exports. Similarly, Singapore has very few tariff barriers or discriminatory policy against imports from India. The UAE has not defined its anti-dumping policy clearly but discriminatory measures are very much prevalent against Indian exports. Tariff rates range from 0% - 4%.

The NTBs in the Russian market include subsidies on food products, life saving drugs, agro chemicals, special purchases by defence and other critical sectors. Customs duties range from 0% - 200% and customs clearance charges are 0.15% *ad valorem* in addition to special taxes on import (1.5%) and value added tax (20%). There is restriction regarding export of items from India with high import content under rupee account.

Bangladesh has tariff rates ranging from 7.5% - 50% and NTBs such as anti-dumping. Saudi Arabia considered as India's fourteenth largest market has tariff ranging from 0% - 20%. The trade regime is liberal though some items are banned on religious grounds. Import regulation is discriminatory against India for drugs, pharmaceuticals, marine products and meat.

Thailand, which figures as the fifteenth largest market, has reduced duty rates from 100% to 30% since January 1995. The NTBs include restricted imports of agriculture commodities.

3.3 BARRIERS TO EXPORT AT THE MICRO LEVEL

Recognition of the contribution by non traditional exports to Industrial development, led Governments to create institutions and programmes to encourage private sector activity towards export diversity. However, trade barriers to export development remain.

Many of the barriers stem from inadequate Government policies and regulations, lack of suitable export infrastructure or difficulties concerning access to foreign markets.

Dymsza (1983) observed that the essential element in development of national export strategy was identification of the obstacles facing industrial development. He identified them as unrealistic exchange rates, inadequate export infrastructure and cumbersome export procedures, in addition to the primary obstacle of import substitution policy as major barriers to export.

A microeconomic approach would help uncover means by which the private sector can support export promotion. Several research studies in developing countries of Latin America and elsewhere identified the following export barriers :

- Rational and behavioural factors
- Premature entry into Export due to GATT incentives
- Export Supply problems
- Firm Specific Problems (as managerial capacity)
- Export Demand Problems (lack of knowledge about markets)
- Transport and communications
- Packaging and labelling
- Export Documentation
- Availability of and cost of export insurance
- Transportation Insurance
- Transport Services, infrastructure
- Customs requirements—local and foreign (changing regulations)
- Bilateral Agreements—government to government often disregards private interests
- Market information—Bulk of it to come from own sources
- Need to change internal culture of companies to export mentality
- Product Design and Specification
- Methods of market entry and expansion (channel choice, local agencies)
- Product Competitiveness (depends on exchange rate and managerial capacity of exporters)
- Lack of Continuity in government economic policies

- Foreign Government Policy
- Competition between domestic and export oriented industries

Basic problems like currency exchange, transport infrastructure, and customs expectation are to be dealt with, before private sector industries could be successful. Three needs have been established.

1. Information provision
2. Exporter Education
3. Organisational Support

Information Provision deficiencies exist in the area of financial information and market information. Credit and capacity assessment of prospective buyers are found wanting for commercial banks and other private agencies. Market information from public sector organisations are largely ineffectual. Private business organisations should plan to provide relevant, current and timely information; at a nominal cost as individual market research could be out of reach of small companies.

Private sector, along with chambers of commerce, industrial associations and business schools could offer training in export documentation, customs procedures, transport and financial requirements, countertrade and studying opportunities in new markets.

Luis (1982) indicates that although many export and trade institutions have been established, further research may be needed to evaluate the effectiveness of these institutions. Programmes to alleviate the problems of barriers to export need the support of a continuous, long term government policy, a proactive approach from business organisations and educational institutions and individual business' reliance on self help.

The above comments would apply to most of the developing countries, especially to a country like India. Of course, many of the barriers, are being tackled under one or the other strategy, but the efficacy of the programmes are to be continuously monitored.

Studies in other parts of the world, both developed and developing, surprisingly exhibit similarities such as lack of market and customer information, difficulty in finding distributors and concerns about competitiveness. With more time allocation and assistance, company barriers can be overcome, while tariff and non-tariff barriers are to be lived with. Higher costs and risks are to be factored into company's decisions. Government can to some extent, assist in overcoming the barriers but many are to be tackled at company level.

As small scale exports contribute to over 40% of India's exports, the intensity of such barriers would be higher and promotional activities have to be aimed at small and medium scale exporters.

The effect of many of the barriers at micro level could be assuaged by government export promotion programs aimed at specific areas such as :

- Advertising, local seminars (highlighting benefits of exports) to meet motivational barriers.
- Market reviews, overseas visits, collection and dissemination of market data to meet informational barriers.
- Bid operations and trade fair participation reduces the burden of new and expanding exporters. This would combat operational and resource based barriers.

Export promotion works best when the programs offered and used closely match the needs of the companies. Role of non-governmental and business associations is to be complementary to government and programs should avail services of international organisations like UNCTAD and WTO.

3.4 THE WORLD TRADE ORGANISATION

The world trading system is undergoing vast changes under the influence of 'multilaterism' and 'regionalism'. These seemingly opposing trends of free trade and preferential trade liberalisation is the subject of debate as to the final outcome. The world is today witnessing an increasing number of regional economic integration like NAFTA, EU, AFTA, APEC and SAPTA while concurrently professing free trade.

The Uruguay round accord signed at the end of seven long years of negotiation since 1986 reflects the interest of countries at different stages of development in the area of international trade. Though it is likely to impact different countries at different intensities with certain lobbies vehemently protesting against the accord, it is the best possible defence against increasing unilaterism and protectionism in international trade. As markets for developing country manufactured goods are in developed nations, tariff reductions are of interest to exporters in developing countries. Nations realise that adjustment to free trade may initially be painful (by having to liberalise domestic markets), in the long run both developed and developing nations are sure to benefit. It is therefore not surprising that many more developing countries are seriously advocating membership (PRC, Taiwan, CIS).

Future rounds could see areas of controversy in environmental issues, labour standards and mobility, but a sensible strategy for WTO could be to make overall gains broad enough to enable each negotiating country to accept gains that outweigh losses. Freedom of developing countries to enjoy special and differential treatment is likely to be eroded and developed countries may have to conform to practices in developed countries. Imposition of social and regulatory standards will be particularly controversial. Demands by Developed Countries would be made to raise safety, occupational and environmental standards in developing countries.

3.4.1 Implications for Developing Countries

With the establishment of a multilateral trading system, the major influences likely to be faced by developing countries are :

- The regulatory framework of WTO
- The growth of regional trading blocs
- Evolution towards a managed trading system
- Development of deeper economic integration

All the above scenarios would likely lead to increased obligations by developing countries. Over the years, many developing countries were able to obtain exemptions from GATT regulations, the future will see this relaxation of obligations on a decreasing scale. Whatever the final outcome, developing countries should rely on export-led growth, despite the fact the different scenarios will affect them differently, even if terms of trade may worsen in the short term, and some markets may seem to be protected. Manufactured goods exports from developing countries have increased despite a general decline in import growth in developed markets (Exports of textiles and shoes have grown in spite of quota constraints). As developing country exports are still a small percentage of developed markets, the direction of exports of manufactured goods could only be positive.

3.4.2 WTO : Implications for Indian Exports

The WTO, which came into being on Jan.1, 1995, after prolonged negotiations under the Uruguay rounds, is expected to lead to further liberalisation of international trade. The Uruguay rounds moved beyond the traditional concerns of earlier GATT into various new areas like Trade Related Intellectual Property Rights (TRIPS), Trade Related Investment Measures (TRIMS) and trade in services. The various terms of agreement likely to have impact on India's exports are tariffs, antidumping measures, subsidies, countervailing duties and agriculture.

Tariffs

The reduction in global tariff as a result of market access negotiations, would imply greater opportunities to Indian exports though the impact on exports to developed countries may be nominal as their tariff level is low at present (5-6%; likely to be reduced to 3-4%). Of much more benefit would be WTO's ability to limit non-tariff barriers.

Non-tariff Barriers

Anti-dumping measures or safeguard measures which are major non-tariff barriers for entry into developed markets would in future be restricted. Indian exports of steel ropes, wires and rods were the target of such protectionist measures in the past. Indian exports are likely to benefit qualitatively more than quantitatively because of this.

Export Subsidies

Though the GATT agreement prohibits subsidies including direct tax exemptions, impact on countries like India with per capita income below US$ 1000 or 3.25% of world exports would be minimal. Indian exports of gems and jewellery alone would be affected by this prohibition against subsidies.

Agriculture

Developing countries need to reduce level of support to

agriculture if the aggregate measure of support (AMS) exceeds 10%. India need not have to reduce support (as the AMS is below 6%) in the short and medium term. Further, as a developing country with BOP problems, India need not have any market access commitments for agriculture and incentives like tax exemptions under 80 HHC do not attract requirements of reduction. India is therefore internationally competitive in many agricultural products (in addition to tea, coffee and spices) and further policy liberalisation could benefit agricultural exports such as rice, cotton and wheat.

Textiles and Garments

India stands to gain from the phasing out of MFA in ten years. During the next decade, Indian exporters could develop competitiveness in products in which they enjoy comparative advantage (cotton and cotton blended textiles) and benefit during the post MFA period, though it is likely to be very competitive.

Service Sector

Liberalisation of the service sector like finance and banking along with cross border movement of personnel holds potential for considerable gain in areas like software, construction, consultancy and medical services.

Trade Related Investment Measures (TRIMS)

TRIMS which tries to remove restrictions on FDI or reduce ceiling on foreign equity holding does not affect India's foreign investment policy in any manner.

Trade Related Intellectual Property Rights (TRIPS)

Though India currently recognises only processed patents (in chemicals, pharmaceuticals, veterinary products and food products), it may necessarily have to recognise product patents in future. Foreign manufacturers holding monopolistic position in drugs and pharmaceuticals may increase drug prices. As the Uruguay round agreement recognises patenting of plant and seed varieties which may increase prices of new varieties of plants and seeds, India may have to resort to 'Sui Generis' system of protection for holders of plant breeders rights in case of commercial production and marketing. Indian farmers may develop and use seeds for their own operations. It is however inevitable that developed countries with high investment in R&D may benefit from the large number of patents held. Low proportion of drugs in use under patents, the special pricing policy of MNC's in developing countries and exports of Indian drugs mostly unpatented may be in India's favour.

Overall Impact

Strengthening of the multilateral trading process may protect weaker countries which are subject to bilateralism and regionalism. GATT principles of transparency, predictability, non-discrimination, fair trading rules and MFN based trade would indeed be helpful to Indian exports. India's share of incremental exports as a result of the WTO agreement is estimated between $1.5 billion to $2 billion by the ministry of Commerce. The benefits may echo during the course of the coming decade. The exporters, policy makers and concerned organisations have the time gap within which to implement various preparatory measures to exploit the opportunities the future holds.

3.4.3 Major Concerns Arising Out of WTO

- Acceptance of pharmaceutical (product) patents which push up drug prices, and deprive those who cannot afford them of life saving medicines.
- Farmers will be forced to pay royalties for new improved varieties of agricultural seeds, whether or not these arise from biotechnology patents.

- Back end loading of phased elimination of MFA, may delay access to textile and garment markets of US and EU.

Despite these concerns, an overall increase in India's exports could be the likely outcome under the WTO. Sir Michael Perry CBE. Chairman Unilever, observed that India has to go through a learning curve like other developing exporting countries of Asia. India cannot pigeon hole itself as a producer of bargain basement goods at cheap labour prices.

Therefore the next decade, within which a freer world trading system is envisaged, government and business should gear up to face intense international competition by raising the quality of human capital (through education and training), upgrade industry by improving infrastructure and investing heavily in research and development.

3.5 SOUTH ASIAN PREFERENTIAL TRADE AGREEMENT (SAPTA)

The beginning of 1966, saw the SAARC (South Asian Association for Regional Co-operation, of which India, Bhutan, Bangla-Desh, Maldives, Nepal, Pakistan and Sri Lanka are members) commerce ministers discuss trade among the member countries and implementation of SAPTA, to be followed by second round of negotiations at Colombo. The January 1996 talks concentrated more on co-ordinating trade rather than increasing the quantum. Other areas focused were transit trade, co-ordination of transport and harmonisation of product classification system. Controversial Issues such as barriers to border trade, physical fencing of borders and telecom co-ordination were left out, including issue of non-tariff barriers.

The SAARC fair accompanying the talks attracted

participants from all member countries and did reiterate the fact that member countries produced similar products. The minister of trade from Sri Lanka, Mr. Kingsly Wickramaratne observed that collaboration is the only way to increase SAARC trade.

India's commerce minister Pranab Mukerjee called for a South Asia Free Trade Zone, comprising of SAARC countries. "South Asia cannot develop without mutual co-operation."

This thought was reflected by the business too. Mr. Moshed Khan, chairman of Dacca based Pacific Group of companies observed that "We can't work around one another. We have to work together."

The eight SAARC summit at Delhi on May 4th, 1995, saw an agreement to initiate the South Asian Preferential Trade Agreement (SAPTA). India had offered tariff concessions on 106 items, Pakistan on 35, Sri Lanka on 31, Maldives on 17, Bangladesh on 12 and Bhutan on 7 items. India's offer, viewed in the background of its liberalisation policy and scope of WTO, may not be much economically but will make the neighbours happy as members would like to export to a larger market that India offers.

SAARC, though containing 20% of world population has a share of 1.3% of total world's GDP and its share of world's exports is very very low. Many are the bilateral issues, mostly political which restrain closer relationship (as Mr. J.N. Dixit described this region "as an area of darkness") in political, social and economic co-operation, bypassed by development in world economy.

India's export to SAARC amounts to a small percentage of its total exports, while imports amount to 1%. The potential for increased trade is immense, but hampered by infra-structural inadequacies. India has to instil confidence among the smaller SAARC members, by offering dispensations. As India runs a bilateral surplus with most of the members, this should be possible. The bond of free trade and investment through South Asian Free Trade Area (SAFTA), can lead the nations towards regional integration. Perhaps a SAFTA in over the medium term, if the members are able to surmount innumerable political barriers.

Nearly 58% of India's trade with SAARC countries is accounted for by Bangladesh, followed by Sri Lanka (23%), Nepal (11%) and Pakistan (6%). During 1996-97, India exported Rs. 2912.41 worth of goods to Bangladesh, Rs. 1,668.65 crore to Sri Lanka, Rs. 587.21 crore to Nepal, Rs. 557.83 crore to Pakistan, Rs. 78.3 crore to Bhutan and Rs. 36.79 crore to Maldives. The value of imports from these countries stood at Rs. 220.90 crore, Rs. 160.33 crore, Rs. 227.45 crore, Rs. 128.35 crore, Rs. 54.23 crore and Rs. 0.61 crores respectively. The SAARC nations in 1996-97 made up 5.0% of India's total exports and 0. 60% of imports. In 1990-91, these amounted to 2.9% and 0.41% respectively.

India mainly exports spices, chemicals, engineering products and cotton yarn and fabrics to Bangladesh, spices, oil meals and iron ore to Pakistan, spices and cotton fabrics and made-ups to Sri Lanka and raw tobacco to Nepal. India's imports include raw jute, urea and newsprint from Bangladesh, tea from Sri Lanka and dry fruits from Pakistan.

While the government is hopeful that the SAPTA would lead to a SAFTA within a few years, there are sceptics who feel that the process would take much longer. They point out that the first round of negotiations covering 225 tariff lines account for a meagre 6.2% of the total value of intra-regional trade. Covering the remaining 92-93 per cent would call for protracted negotiations. Also, with the exception of Sri Lanka, none of the other members are likely to welcome India's proposal for a SAFTA by 2000. At best, they would agree to a 2005 AD schedule, but India has recently insisted that the change should be brought about by 2001.

3.6 EUROPEAN UNION (EU)

As a major economic group, the EU accounts for nearly 38% of world trade. The combined population of the fifteen member countries is 372 million with a total GDP of ECU 7080 billion and imports of US$ 706.1 billion in 1997. (EIU country report 1997-98). As countries of East and Central Europe along with Greece and Turkey are likely to be admitted as members, in future, the European Union holds very high potential for Indian exports.

India's foreign trade to the EU has been progressively increasing but is characterised by a continuing trade deficit. The composition includes engineering goods, garments, leather manufacturers, drugs and pharmaceuticals, handicrafts, carpets, jewellery and food articles all of which constitute 70% of India's exports to Europe.

European Union, under its Mediterranean policy has established special economic and trade relations with the Mediterranean region and products originating from these countries enjoy duty and quota free entry into the union. Any manufacturing facility set up by Indian businessmen in the Mediterranean region could benefit from this policy.

Similarly, 70 African, Caribbean and Pacific countries (ACP) are signatories to the Lome convention whose products enjoy privileged access to the EU. Manufacturing in the Lome member countries from raw materials sourced from India could help easy access to the EU markets.

Several of the EU consumers are attuned to Indian products and offer prospective growth areas. India's share in imports of UK (0.58%), Germany (0.31%), Netherlands (0.28%), France (0.19%) and Italy (0.3%) are indeed low and need focused promotional support. Eastern Germany and Portugal (low wage countries) may also offer scope for setting up manufacturing bases. Similarly, countries of Central and East Europe who are likely to be members of EU in future may also be targeted for establishing manufacturing bases.

3.7 NORTH AMERICAN FREE TRADE AREA (NAFTA)

NAFTA, comprising of Canada, USA and Mexico, accounting for 21.3% of world trade is the largest free trade zone in the world. The population totals 359.75 million and the combined GDP is estimated US$ 6.77 trillion, with imports aggregating US$ 1078 billion and exports to US$ 920 billion in 1996. Countries of South America are likely to be admitted as members, the ultimate goal being a free trade area of the Americas. US is India's biggest market, but Mexico's cheap labour combined with US capital may pose increased competition to Indian products. NAFTA currently accounts for 22% of India's exports of textiles including garments.

The strategy to succeed in the largest consumer market—US, is to attract US investment in India for export to US as well as setting up manufacturing base in Mexico for duty free entry into US markets. Indian exports to Mexico have been showing a healthy increase since 1991-92.

3.8 ASSOCIATION OF SOUTH EAST ASIAN NATIONS (ASEAN)

Out of the seven member nations of ASEAN, Indonesia, Philippines and Singapore offers scope for joint ventures. As fast growing economies, they offer attractive targets for trade, investment and tourism. India should strive to improve trade relations with ASEAN as currently, she is accepted as a dialogue member.

Name	Pop.	Labour	Capital	Natural Resources
1 China-Burma-Laos-Thailand (Golden Quadrangle)	47m	Thailand, Yunnan	Thailand	Laos, Burma
2 Indonesia-Malaysia-Thailand (Growth Triangle)	22m	Northern Sumatra	Penang	Southern Thailand
3 Indonesia-Malaysia-Singapore (Growth Triangle)	5.3m	Batam/Johor (limited)	Singapore	
4. Southern China (Growth Triangle)	88m	Guangdong	Hong Kong and Taipei	Limited
5. East ASEAN (Growth Polygon)	40m	All except Brunei	Brunei	All

The ASEAN has a total population of 321 million and a GNP of $321 billion. India's share of imports into Malaysia (0.6%), Indonesia (0.5%) and Singapore (0.6%) is quite modest, though showing an upward trend. New growth zones have been identified which do not fall into formal regional trade blocks, but include countries both within ASEAN and outside around Asia.

3.9 ASIA PACIFIC ECONOMIC CO-OPERATION (APEC)

Asia Pacific Economic Co-operation (APEC) was initiated in 1989 as a forum for informal discussion within the region. Today, eighteen countries forming APEC (accounting for 60% of world's domestic product and 40% of its trade) range from developed and developing countries around the Asia Pacific basin. An agreement signed in November 1994, holds a broad based vision for economic co-operation. The combined GDP totalled an astounding US$ 10,640 billion with individual GDP ranging between US$ 5 billion (Brunei) and US$ 5446 billion (USA). Exports from APEC totalled US$ 2183 billion and imports US$2347 billion in 1996.These figures indicate the magnitude and importance of APEC.

The Seoul Declaration of 1991, sets out the objectives of APEC as follows:

(1) To sustain the growth and development of the region and contribute to the development of the world economy.

(2) To enhance the positive gains resulting from increasing economic interdependence by encouraging flow of goods, services, capital and technology.

(3) To develop and strengthen the open multilateral trading system.

(4) To reduce barriers to trade in goods, services and investment among participants in a manner consistent with GATT principles.

The Declaration also specified that APEC was to encourage private sector participation in APEC activities. APEC further supports 'open regionalism' to encourage trade liberalisation throughout the world economy.

Other goals set out for the APEC were :

- Harmonisation of standards such as measures.
- Investment code offering minimum protection to investors against nationalisation and allowing repatriation of profits.
- An effective end to dual tax.
- An arbitration panel for settling disputes.

Among measures planned include cutting of bureaucratic red tape such as customs rules, reduce tariffs with a view to strengthen existing economic links between North America and East Asia. APEC is likely to become the biggest and potentially most influential trade grouping in the world.

APEC will in all probability find itself competing with other regional groups such as Association of South East Asian Nations (ASEAN), East Asian Economic Caucus (EAEC), Pacific Trade and Development Conference (PAFTAD), Pacific Basin Economic Co-operation (PBEC) and Pacific Economic Co-operation Council (PECC). Competition from EAEC is likely to be stronger as it includes Asian members of the APEC. However, suggestions have been made that EAEC could exist as a lose consultation forum within the framework of APEC.

India could benefit from a successful APEC if it is able to develop better trade relations with members of ASEAN who could help establish Indian products in the developed markets of APEC. Production facilities, if established in Asian countries of APEC, could assist India's exports of intermediaries and other inputs. India already enjoys a good relationship as dialogue partner of ASEAN.

3.10 SHOULD INDIA JOIN A TRADING BLOC?

Since the end of World War II, the world witnessed two waves of regional trading arrangements (deMELO and Panagriya, 1992). The first wave spread through Africa, Latin America and other parts of the developing world, motivated by different economic rationale (Bhagwati, 1992) such as exploiting economies of scale through regional arrangements. The second wave started in the mid eighties in North America, Europe as well as the Asia Pacific.

The world trading system may soon be divided into four blocs (Bhagwati & Srinivasan,1993), the expanding European Union, the NAFTA extending into South America and Pan-Asian Bloc and a bloc of nations that are not part of any of the three blocs. India, if it does not join any one of the blocs, may have to face trade barriers posed by all the three blocs.

In their paper (1992), Mr. Sanjbib Pohit of the NCAER and Mr. Rajiv Chada of Hindu College used Global Trade Analysis Package (GTAP) developed by Professor Thomas W. Herlet of Perdue University, West Lafayette to analyse the impact of South Asia joining various blocs on trade, welfare, resource allocation, etc. India was not an independent element but included as part of South Asia. Out of six experiments conducted by them, the maximum benefit will accrue if South Asia has a preferential trade agreement with EU, followed by an agreement with NAFTA.

3.11 CONCLUSION

Retrospection would show that Indian exports had to face

a number of barriers at the micro and macro levels. Removal of these barriers would require careful and dispassionate identification of the barriers and formulation of necessary measures. Further, major trade groups around the world are a reality. India will have to evolve a suitable international trade policy within the framework of a dynamic foreign policy so as to be able to derive maximum possible advantage from these trade groups.

CHAPTER 4

EXPORT PROMOTION AROUND THE WORLD

4.1 INTRODUCTION

There seems to be a wide variance in the export promotion strategies formulated and implemented around the world. An overview of the strategies in selected countries follows. First, attention has been focused on export promotion strategies in developed countries followed by examination of export promotion strategies in some Asian countries.

A panapoly of different policy instruments impact on export activities, some more directly than others. Export policy instruments may operate on supply side (initiatives for creating and expanding export production, transport networks, port facilities, financial, tax and investment systems). Demand side policies attempt to stimulate more sales through promotional methods.

Government often influences export activity and performance through shaping :

- Overall economic infrastructure
- Specific industrial structures
- Development of individual companies

The role of non-government organisations is complementary to government departments and export development requires a co-operative approach and institutions which are directly or indirectly linked with government.

The future trends and directions point towards intensifying international competition, changes in the role and scale of government, increasing knowledge of how companies internationalise, more sophisticated export marketing, more open markets and freer trade, increasing manufacturing capabilities in developing world, shorter product life cycles, converging consumer tastes and technology advances. This would entail further challenges to government in increased export promotion budgets.

4.2 EXPORT PROMOTION IN DEVELOPED COUNTRIES

Developed countries, despite their higher share in world exports, do have governmental and private programmes in support of their exports. The objective of these programmes is generally to expand exports of particular products as also to develop regional industrial growth. In this part, export promotion strategies of Canada, UK, Italy, West Germany and France are briefly examined.

4.2.1 Canada

The two export promotion institutions are Department of Regional Industrial Expansion (DRIE) and the Department of External Affairs (DEA). Nineteen priority markets were identified by DEA for export focus and its export market development program offers risk sharing between government and business in new market ventures. It offers support for companies participating in trade fairs, exhibitions and the like.

Most of the organisations involved in Canadian export promotion are public enterprises, concentrating on export information and advisory activities, less on marketing support. Only the Export Development Corporation is involved in finance and guarantees.

4.2.2 United Kingdom

Britain has few organisations to promote exports like Italy and Singapore. The British Overseas Trade Board (BOTB) has commercial counsellors stationed around the world and assist small and medium sized companies through trade fairs, exhibition assistance, advisory services and the Export Intelligence Service.

The Export Credit Guarantee Department provides export guarantees and purchaser credits. The National Economic Development Office (NEDO) operates an advisory body that discusses UK trade problems and policies. Majority of UK organisations concentrate on export marketing activities, though financial efforts are limited to financing trade fairs.

4.2.3 Italy

Italian export promotion is directed towards providing marketing and financial support, mostly from Italian Banks.

Export Promotion activities are centred around the Ministry of Foreign Trade (MFT) and its Instituto per il Commercio Estero (ICE) which offers training programs, information services, trade fairs and publishes journals and information bulletins.

The 94 Chambers of Commerce in Italy and 40 Chambers of Commerce established overseas assist in promotion of Italian trade. The Italian Organisation of Industry and employees assist in export collaboration to form export consortia.

4.2.4 West Germany

Most export promotion and trade assistance are channelled through private organisations, as the government values free market economy. Export promotion support is mostly used by small and medium sized companies, while some educational and advisory services are available only to small companies.

The Ausfuhrkredit - Gesellschaft m.b:h (AKA) provides short and medium term loans, while the state development Bank Kreditansalt fur Wiederanfbau (KFU) provides long term financing and consultancy. Hermes Kreditvrsicherings Aktien gesellsehaft A.G provides guarantees and insurance policies on behalf of the government.

There is minimal governmental export promotion and limited interaction between export promotion and other policies. No Special Tax Concessions are available for exporters.

4.2.5 France

Trade promotion and assistance are provided mainly by Government Institutions in informational and advisory services as well as support for production, marketing and finance and guarantees, focused on small and medium sized firms.

The Direction des Relation Economiques E Y Terieures (DREE) is a policy - making organisation, which negotiates bilateral trade agreements and multilateral trade policy activities. The Centre Francais du Commerce Exterieure (CFCE) publishes market studies, export regulations and informational journals. The Agence pour la Co-operation Technique Industrielle et Economique (ACTIM) provides support to consulting firms in the form of feasibility studies. Export marketing support is provided by Comite Francais des Manifestation Economiques a l'Etranger (CFMEE) and the Compagnie pour le Financement de Stock a l'Etranger (LOFICE) assists participation at trade fairs.

France has an extensive and well developed system of export credit and guarantees, well serviced by banks, in addition to a comprehensive co-ordinated trade promotion program.

Special tax concessions for foreign investment and development assistance, financial support for research and development are available. The ANBAR organisation extends interest free loans for overseas market research and technical development, and the loan becomes non-repayable (up to specific amount) if the venture fails.

The French trade promotion program is very broad and extensive and is well co-ordinated with France's administration, the banking system and enterprise.

A study of several developed economies suggests that form of assistance and its co-ordination varies among countries. Wide divergence's do not necessarily produce divergent outcomes—as proved by West Germany and Japan which are both successful exporters despite totally different orientations.

4.3 EXPORT PROMOTION IN DEVELOPING COUNTRIES

Policy Considerations

It is indeed preferable, for developing countries to accelerate their growth process by means of export promotion (Little, Scitovsky and Scott 1970). It has been demonstrated that countries pursuing export oriented policies attained faster growth in both exports and GNP, had higher domestic savings and experienced greater gain in total factor productivity (RICDEZ). However the openness of the economy for Foreign Investment and Imports, not export growth alone, was found to be a critical ingredient of growth. Open policies also help adapting to quickly changing technologies around the world. Imports are expected to provide access to technology and capital goods while exports help exploit the comparative advantage in resources. An export promotion strategy creates a demand driven stimulation to income and output in the economy and benefits from economies of scale due to larger market size.

Till the 1970's, the dominant thinking in developing countries was to encourage the infant industries achieve self sufficiency through industrialisation, under restrictive trade practices, complex import licensing and quota system, stringent foreign exchange controls, overvalued currency and regulations on foreign investments. The 1980's and 1990's saw developing countries rationalising and liberalising their trade regimes with the help of World Bank and International Monetary Fund. It has to be noted that liberalisation policies in many developing countries were pursued unilaterally without any reciprocal concessions from developed countries, or due commitments under multilateral agreements like GATT.

4.4 EXPORT PROMOTION IN SOME ASIAN COUNTRIES

During the past decade, very significant changes have occurred in some of the Asian countries in the field of export promotion. Since an attempt is being made in the present work to evolve some feasible and effective export promotion strategies for India, it will be worthwhile to draw upon the experience of some of our Asian brethren. Hence, in the following part, the export promotion endeavours in Japan, South Korea, Singapore, PRC, Hong Kong, Taiwan, Malaysia, Thailand, Indonesia and Pakistan are examined.

4.4.1 Japan

Export promotion ranges from export planning, production and marketing to finance guarantees. Japan alone devotes promotion effort to product development for overseas markets.

Ministry of International Trade and Industry (MITI) and Japan External Trade Organisation (JETRO) are the primary government institutions offering a full range of export services—officiating as policy maker and operational body.

Export-Import Bank of Japan operating as an independent body provides a variety of financial services to exporters and importers. The Overseas Economic Co-operation Fund (OECF) provides funds in cases where Export-Import Bank is unable to help.

The Federation of Japanese Industries (KEIDANREN) which is a combination of nine largest trading houses, banks and industrial enterprises controlling more than half of Japan's exports, takes an active role in export promotion.

4.4.2 South Korea

The success of Korean outward oriented trade policy was dependent on an educated work force, good transport and communication, macroeconomic stability and leadership provided by the government. Close co-operation between the government and the Chaebols (general trading companies) and the banks have helped promote South Korea's export.

An export subsidy route to outward orientation helped rapid economic growth and industrialisation. The finance sector was used to favour selected industries or projects. On the domestic side, agriculture, chemicals and consumer industries were highly protected. While many imports were exempt from duties, others were subject to prohibitive tariffs. Import of raw materials and non-competitive intermediate goods were approved almost automatically.

The preferential tax system for exporters included

tariff exemption on raw materials and intermediates and capital goods, exemption from indirect taxes on inputs and export sales, reduction of direct taxes on profits, preferential loan system for short and long term loans, generous wastage allowance and preferential rates on overheads (electricity, railroad transportation). In addition, exporters received immense administrative support.

Primary focus of export promotion activities is on marketing support, followed by export information and advisory services. Exim Bank of South Korea, provides direct loans, finance for market studies, direct investments abroad and trading expenses overseas.

The Ministry of Commerce and Industry (MCI), the principal government agency works closely with private enterprises through the Korean Traders Association (KTA) and the Korean Trade Promotion Corporation (KOTRA).

4.4.3 Singapore

Focus of export promotion is on export information and advice and marketing. The Export Development Board (EDB) and the Trade Development Board (TDB) are the two primary Export Promotion Organisations. EDB offers assistance's for MNC's to establish in Singapore, through its headquarters and fifteen other offices overseas.

Trade Development Board, funded by the government, provides export information, advisory services and marketing support. Export financing and guarantees are provided by Export Credit Insurance Corporation of Singapore. The Singapore Chinese Chamber of Commerce provides local contacts, while the Singapore International Chamber of Commerce (private) provides export planning support through information and contacts. Intraco, a private company, assists small companies. It assists in export marketing assistance, in the form of marketing information and product development advice with a fewer organisations but close co-operation between them. Singapore has developed a co-ordinated trade promotion program.

4.4.4 People's Republic of China (PRC)

The important factors influencing Export Promotion which are rather common to all developing countries are:

Technology Transfer

PRC is extremely eager to obtain technology through buying , license, know-how, high tech components and productive equipment. The methods are complex—joint ventures, with buy back guarantees, counterpurchase and other forms of countertrade. As regards foreign currency-PRC has been adjusting its policies from time to time.

Poor Infrastructure

PRC's railways are well-developed but telecommunications, electricity and skill of labour indeed represent weak areas.

Regional Approach

PRC has focused on coastal provinces and fourteen Special Economic Zones (SEZ) offering tax rebates, but retaining autonomy in sourcing employees, raw materials etc.

Economic Reforms

Export door (especially agriculture, industry and services) is more widely open than for import. Decentralisation of decision making on economic matters has been pushed from state to provincial to municipal levels.

Against the key background factors, the policy instruments to push exports are:

Joint Ventures have been actively encouraged though a good percentage of these are with Hong Kong and other overseas Chinese, followed by Japanese, European and US firms. Joint ventures have to export all their production.

PRC is using various countertrade devices (barter, countertrade, coproduction) to save on foreign exchange and gain access to international markets.

Subcontracting

It is realised that subcontracting to MNC's can help technology transfer and hard currency acquisition, though MNC's are wary of quality control.

Foreign Currency Retention

Increasingly Joint Ventures and domestic concerns are permitted to retain for their use, a portion of foreign exchange earned by them.

Enterprise Autonomy

Management of enterprises are progressively allowed more say in business decisions.

Trade Fairs and Overseas Trade Representatives

International Trade fairs (annually at GUNGCHOW) and a permanent fair at Shanghai are used in trade promotion. Permanent overseas trade representation as well as participation in overseas fairs are encouraged.

Tourism

It is considered as a high priority area and overseas investors are encouraged to invest in hotels and tourism infrastructure.

Overseas businesses are expected to plan three, six or ten year strategies in establishing contacts with relevant community, institutions and authorities. Despite the hurdles, PRC offers pleasant surprises at both personal, professional and business levels.

Often, the PRC, since 1978 is held as a role model for India, partly due to the similarities in their history and economic development. However, China has forged ahead much faster than India in many spheres. What explains China's surging ahead? China has been in reforms much longer—since 1978 and has been effective in relying on overseas Chinese network for capital, skills and contacts. This is in contrast to the non-resident Indians who were until recently, viewed with suspicion. Further, China transformed centre-state relations, allowing regional specialisation and faster growth in the coastal provinces.

4.4.5 Hong Kong

Hong Kong enjoys a unique position in international trade because of its geographical position, free port status and government policy of 'positive non-intervention'. Only few products like petroleum, alcohol, tobacco are subject to import tariffs. This has helped Hong Kong to develop itself as an international business centre and is ranked as eighth largest exporter in the world. As an entreport, re-exports currently account for 60% of its total exports. Hong Kong is ranked as the fifth largest destination for Indian products and India's export trade with Hong Kong is likely to go up. The Trade Development Council which is an independent body responsible for development of Hong Kong's export is financially supported by the Government.

4.4.6 Taiwan

Taiwan experienced rapid economic growth since the 60's accompanied by greater equity in income distribution. The government policy preferred trade liberalisation and export promotion at an equilibrium exchange rate plus a market determined interest rate to ensure maximisation of voluntary savings and efficient allocation of capital funds. In the late 50's, Taiwan government devalued the

NT dollar against the USD, reduced budget deficits, liberalised selected imports, simplified protection offsets, all of which led to rapid expansion of foreign trade in the 1960's. Import substitution policies were continued and domestic prices were higher than world market prices. Export incentives were used to offset high cost of production for exports. Low inflation and stable effective exchange rates, devaluation by more than 60% and protection offset (16%) were effective in realising higher export targets. Subsequently, import restrictions were reduced to contain inflation.

4.4.7 Malaysia

Malaysia is ranked as the world's 19th largest trading nation with exports totalling US$ 78.4 billion in 1996 with manufacturing exports accounting for 70% of total exports.

India's exports to Malaysia had shown a steady progress (Rs. 899 crores in 1994-95) and Rs. 1885 crores in 1996-97, while imports were higher (Rs. 3697 crores in 1996-97). India's exports include traditional and non-traditional items like tea, coffee, rice, spices, cashew, leather and leather manufactures and gems and jewellery. India had entered into 42 joint ventures in Malaysia till 1994 and in recent years, Malaysia too had established several joint ventures in India.

Both countries had signed several trade and investment agreements in 1995 for co-operation in proposed super highway project as well as in investment guarantee. Agreements were also signed in joint development of satellite communications and in space and telecommunications research.

Due to Malaysia's prominent role in ASEAN, India would benefit from better trade and investment agreements with Malaysia.

4.4.8 Thailand

The Thai economy grew steadily since the 50's on agriculture based exports. Moderate protection in some sectors (for revenue purposes) sheltered Thai firms from international competition. But increased production and competition reduced domestic prices to international levels. Subsidies on credits for exports (which mostly benefited larger firms), devaluation in 1981 and 1984 by about 30%, bonded factories, export processing zones and tight fiscal policy led to expanded exports during the 80's.

4.4.9 Indonesia

Pragmatic economic policies, substantial foreign aid and private capital inflows as well as massive windfall of increased oil prices changed the Indonesian economy during the 70's. In the early 1960's, Indonesia had only a small manufacturing sector among developing countries. Rapid industrialisation aimed at the domestic market under a protectionism regime subsequently helped exports of manufactured goods overtaking traditional agriculture exports.

Major reforms pursued by the Indonesian government after oil prices fell was the adjustment of the exchange rate combined with conservative fiscal and monetary policies. The Rupiah was devalued twice (1983 and 1986) and tied loosely to the USD. Among the micro economic reforms were the duty drawback and exemption on imported inputs. The program was effectively managed and helped exporters of all sizes, locations and industries. Management of the bureaucratic customs was handed over to the Swiss company SGS. However, many NTBs were retained favouring politically powerful business groups. Sweeping modifications of the taxation system followed, banking system was liberalised and foreign investments poured in. Composition of Indonesia's exports reflected its comparative advantage (plywood, fertilisers, paper products, steel products and tyres) which is mostly natural resource based. The success of Indonesian export strategy, in the past has been partly attributed to the political stability.

4.4.10 Pakistan

Pakistan, back in 1947, had little industries, abundant agricultural land, a tiny entrepreneurial class and a per capita income of US$ 100. Since then, Pakistan tried to move towards a more open trading regime and has improved its exports to US$ 7.8 billion by 1995-96. Import substitution policies, a chronic foreign exchange shortage and agriculture based exports were the principal constraints.

Pakistan tried (between 1959 and 1961) an export bonus scheme, rewarding exporters of manufactured goods with import privileges followed by open general license and a free list for imports. During the period 1972-1978, when it lost East Pakistan to Bangladesh, the rupee was devalued and most import licensing and export bonus scheme were removed.

The country suffered a continuous trade deficit as imports kept rising. The price of major exports like cotton yarn, cotton, cotton made garments, bed ware and towels decreased. Major imports were of chemicals, iron and steel, paper, crude oil and petroleum products and led to trade deficits. In 1955, Pakistan introduced a three year tariff reduction program while moving towards a market oriented agriculture policy. To increase competition in textile and clothing industry, concessional credit and dual cotton pricing system was phased out. Access to yarn and cotton substitutes had been improved by allowing imports at reduced tariffs. Removal of textile from the negative list is likely to help export production. Both India and Pakistan would benefit from trade in complementary products if they can surmount the political hurdles.

4.4.11 Sri Lanka

At the time of independence in 1948, Sri Lanka was poised for growth as its national income was higher than other South Asian countries. Weak manufacturing sector and fluctuating prices of agricultural exports led to import controls and an over valued currency.

During 1977-79, liberalisation was ushered in by a shift from quotas to tariffs, devaluation of the rupee, managed float and export assistance measures. A massive investment program financed by foreign aid was taken up. Various export promotion measures such as improved duty drawback schemes partly financed by a cess on imports were set up. Exports were helped by increased demand for garments from quota protected markets. The export promotion measures that began in 1977 seem to have had a long lasting impact.

4.5 EAST ASIAN MIRACLE

The export growth and economic development in East Asia has been remarkable during the past three decades and were often referred to as 'miracles'. At the front of this remarkable growth are the first four 'tigers' namely Hong Kong, Singapore, South Korea and Taiwan. This export growth has been taken up by the second line of tigers—Malaysia Indonesia and which are likely to be followed by Vietnam and others.

Mr. V .V. Bhatt of the World Bank, in his book "East Asian Miracle", 1993 has identified several lessons from the evolution of trade and commercial policy among the developing economies of Asia during the past three decades.

The Asian experience proves that a dynamic export marketing drive had led to a sustained industrialisation in developing countries. This calls for a wide range of trade and exchange policies—such as an exchange rate that reflects the value of foreign exchange earned or saved to the economy—and also specific policies on tariffs, quotas and exchange restrictions—which do not discriminate between production for domestic sales and exports. Most of the successful East Asian countries had realised this and shifted from inward orientation to outward orientation—the NIC's during the 60s, the ASEAN four in the 80s and South Asian countries in late 80s and early 90s.

The high performing Asian Economies have experienced economic inequality and rapid demographic transition. The export oriented growth in an environment of macro economic stability with minimum state intervention is limited to Hong Kong, while state intervention in the form of distortion of prices through various incentives in creating comparative advantage along new lines were the norm in majority of countries. The strategic factors in economic development are a strong commitment to economic development and shared growth assisted by a technocratic, competent bureaucracy, Accumulation of human and physical capital, disciplined national allocation of resources, and adoption, adaptation of modern technology towards improved productivity.

The factors of particular significance included:

- Co-ordination of information exchange
- Receptivity to technological knowledge
- Export promotion or PUSH Co-ordination mechanism.

The East Asian economies encouraged partnership between Government and industry, between Banks and firms, and between regulatory agencies and the Banks, the atmosphere of trust and confidence resulting in reduced transaction cost and risk. Indicative planning provided information on Government objectives which helped decision making by Banks, exporters and other participants.

Technology Policy

The East Asian countries considered technology as an asset, and adopted and adapted diffused as well as accumulated technical knowledge leading to high productivity gain.

Export Push

The Government policies tilted towards export promotion by providing for equipment and technology imports. A transparent yardstick for measurement of Industries, paved the way for Govt. policies on incentives, subsidies and penalties.

But it is the combination of all these strategies and the synergy created which resulted in increasing returns. Many of these strategies and policies can be creatively adapted by other developing countries. The liberalisation of imports should not precede export success, and liberalisation of the financial sector should not imply relaxation of interest rate control or restriction.

4.6 INDIAN MIRACLE?

Between 1965-1990, Asia's twenty three economies grew faster than other regions and these are attributed to sound and stable macro economic policies (getting the fundamentals right) incentives for increasing productivity, openness to foreign ideas and technology, export orientation and development of human resources(with a focus on education).

Active Governmental role, visionary leadership,

commitment to broad based development and an efficient bureaucracy was behind the success. Governments acted as guides and facilitators supporting markets, developing infrastructure and setting framework for policy implementation. Accumulation of human capital was encouraged. International competitiveness was aimed at and private investment was the major vehicle with a focus on communication between Government and business.

4.7 TRANSPLANTING STRATEGIES TO INDIA

The concept of export promotion is as old as trade itself but over the years, export promotion programs have become more comprehensive, sophisticated and innovative.

Despite the similarities in philosophies and strategies, export promotion strategies vary widely from country to country. During the past two decades, developing countries have expanded their exports at twice the growth rate of developed countries, though per capita trade remains low - indicating scope for further growth, especially in manufactured products which have outgrown agricultural exports in the developing countries.

A number of trends are emerging in the export scenario of developing countries such as increasing competition, the changing role of government, globalisation and increasing internationalisation of co-operative business enterprises. This is likely to be accompanied by more open markets, shorter life cycles, converging consumer tastes and technology explosion posing challenges to governments and business.

Can India learn to replicate and emulate the East Asian dragons or transplant strategies successfully elsewhere?

Indian ethos of democracy, individual liberties, and consumerism may not be comparable to countries where political liberty was subservient to economic development. Successful economies evidence factors like culture and attitudes, enterprise and aptitude, supportive socio-political structures as well as institutions and historical circumstances.

India cannot emulate East Asia, but can learn and adapt. Unlike India, East Asia avoided ideological leanings, they emphasised on what worked and policies often addressed economic needs rather than ideology. They avoided prestige products like post graduate education but supported development of primary and secondary education.

The pattern followed the British miracle in the nineteenth century, German and Italian miracle in the 1960s and Japan after the second world war. Today China is at the mid-miracle stage and India is a miracle waiting to happen. Economic miracles do not happen by chance, but call for search, experimentation and reform, and fifty years may be too long for economic policies to be successful. The real issue that needs attention are policies that address basic requirements of growth and fit economy's capacity and environment.

4.7.1 The Chinese Experience

The People's Republic of China has often been quoted as a role model for India because of many similarities in their economies. "Of the six factors identified as causes of China's achievements—four of them—development of non-state sector, the initial emphasis on agriculture development, integration with world economy and the high saving rate could be general lessons for economic reform." (Wing Thye Woo, University of California, May, 1991)

India can emulate China's growth through industrial deregulation and greater integration with the world economy. India should mobilise its private sector to commercialise the agriculture sector with higher productivity. The Indonesian experience confirms that industrialisation and the accompanying higher demand for labour may improve wages and standard of living, and financial discipline of State Owned Enterprises (SOE) without the need for completely dismantling them. China's lesson for India is that a populous country does not necessarily grow slower and a 'Hindu rate of growth' is not unavoidable.

"The case for a liberal economic order that originated with the rise of Korea, Singapore and Taiwan and verified by China and Indonesia in the 1990s, deserves serious consideration by India." (Wing Thye Woo, University of California, May, 1991)

4.7.2 The South Korean Experience

Mr. Lane Taylor, in his lecture at the Indian Investment Centre on April 20, 1994, observed that South Korea has clearly established that the state can effectively intervene in the economy. While examples of Chile, Argentina, Mexico and Turkey suggest that an attempt by authorities not to intervene and turn all decision making over to market can backfire for a variety of reason not confined to economics.

The Korean experience suggests several conclusions relevant to India. The economic bureaucracy had detailed knowledge of the working of the business and was able to practice economic planning as in other countries of South East Asia. The Korean planners co-ordinated economic and industrial policies giving the latter preference. Emphasis was on building production capacity with ample credit creation, selecting and encouraging specific industrial groups, limiting foreign investment to high technology sectors as well as purchase or licensing of technologies under bureaucratic guidance.

Economy of scale was emphasised and competition among Korean firms curtailed. The nationalised banking system extended subsidised loans under priority rationing. The Chaebols, bureaucracy and macro economic policies formed a synergy to develop a creative atmosphere in pushing the economy into overdrive.

4.8 CONCLUSION

A survey of export promotion around the world both in developed and developing economies establishes the need and importance of export promotion though the strategies are as different as the markets themselves. In a fastly changing business world, no strategy could be effective for any length of time and has constantly to be updated to meet the changing circumstances. Experiences of successful economies could serve only as guidelines for policy considerations and not for replication in its entirety.

CHAPTER 5

EXPORT PROMOTION POLICIES, SCHEMES, INCENTIVES AND MEASURES

5.1 INTRODUCTION

With the commencement of planning for economic growth, a need was felt in India to pursue the path of export promotion. With this end in view, India had formulated and implemented a number of dynamic strategies, policies and schemes from time to time in the past. In this chapter, these strategies, policies and schemes have been briefly recapitulated so as to develop a sense of familiarity with export promotion endeavours in India, as well as to provide an adequate backdrop for their critical evaluation in later chapters. In the first part of this chapter dynamic export promotion strategies evolved so far have been described. In the second part, the recent export promotion schemes and incentives have been described followed by review of supporting institutional arrangements.

5.2 REVIEW OF EXPORT PROMOTION STRATEGIES IN INDIA

When economic planning started in India in 1951, the foreign exchange position of the country was quite comfortable, thanks to the accumulation of Sterling Balances in London by the then Government of India during the period of the Second World War. Since the first Five Year Plan was in fact far from being a development plan but was more in the nature of preparation for planning, it envisaged rather modest targets in the various sectors of the economy. Due to this reason, no difficulty in respect of foreign exchange input was felt during the period of the first five year plan. In addition to the fact of accumulated Sterling Balances, India had a big advantage of high export earnings due to the Korean War and the consequent boom in the international economy. However, foreign exchange difficulties started manifesting itself towards the end of the first five year plan and became increasingly apparent with the beginning of the second five year plan.

In the second five year plan, India adopted the strategy of supporting growth of basic heavy industries as a result of Mahalonobis model which not only led to large scale imports of capital goods, but which also created serious scarcity of consumer goods in India. Under the situation, imports increased very fast while the exports grew very marginally due to the microscopic exportable surplus which could be generated, as also due to the composition of India's foreign trade which consisted of mainly primary and unprocessed commodities as well as traditional exportable items like cotton textiles, jute and jute goods, sugar, iron ore, etc. The massive imports of capital goods started during the second five year plan and India faced an acute foreign exchange crisis. It was at this juncture when it was thought necessary to formulate a well considered policy of foreign exchange management based on the tenets of import substitution and export promotion. Though there have been many ups and downs, in this overall thrust, the basic idea remained the same until recently.

5.2.1 Import Substitution and Export Promotion

After the commencement of planning for economic growth in the country, India faced foreign exchange reverses for the first time immediately after the beginning of the Second Five Year Plan in 1958. The problem was so acute that the country was compelled to formulate well considered and active policies of Import Substitution and Export Promotion. Persuant to the policy of Import Substitution, India made efforts in two directions. First, citizens were encouraged to use goods manufactured in India as a substitute for the goods imported from abroad. Second, an effort was made to manufacture in India those goods which were being imported. The country did achieve some success in this matter, though the planners, at that stage, could not visualise the role of imports in a dynamic developing economy. The strategy of import substitution could work well in a static situation in a closed and isolated economy but not in an open and dynamic economy. In an open economy what happens is that due to development process being implemented at an increasing pace, the volume of aggregate imports never declines—only the composition of imports keeps changing depending on the qualitative change in manufactures. This is what happened in India. Thus the strategy of import substitution failed to a certain extent. Subsequently, efforts were made at promoting exports, which too, did not meet with much of a success, as the country could not produce the goods that were in demand in world markets. Again due to population explosion and poor crops, India could not generate much of an exportable surplus of the goods it used to export traditionally. It is well known that world demand for traditional Indian exports has not been supply or price elastic. Due to the action, reaction and interaction of all these variables, only limited success could be achieved in the realm of export promotion.

5.2.2 Export or Perish

Realising that exports should be stepped up substantially

to meet import bill in general and to finance import of food grains and defence equipment (after the war with China in 1962 and with Pakistan in 1965) India switched over to a strategy of Export or Perish during the period of its Fourth Five Year Plan (1969-74) and to do away with the need to go around the world for foreign aid and compromise its national dignity as well as national interest. In 1970 Parliament passed the Export Policy Resolution. During 1972-73, for the first time in many years, a surplus on trade account was recorded. However the oil crisis in 1973 dealt a serious blow to the Indian economy and during 1973-74, the country had a trade deficit of Rs. 432 crore. Thus India could not achieve much of a success with the policy of 'Export or Perish'.

5.2.3 Export More and Import More

With the commencement of the Fifth Five year Plan (1974-79) India adopted the policy of 'Export more and Import more'. As a result of experience with planning for nearly quarter of a century, the planners felt that the country could meet its foreign exchange requirements only when it made serious efforts to export more by importing more. This seems to be the correct approach to export promotion in a dynamic situation which characterised the Indian economy, as borne out by steady rise in exports, imports and balance of trade deficit. The 1990 saw liberalisation of the economy, leading to changes in the export promotion strategies.

5.2.4 Strategy of Liberalised Exports and Imports

With Economic Liberalisation in 1990, India realised that in relation to foreign trade probably the best option was to emulate the South East Asian countries and use foreign trade as an engine of economic growth. India decided to liberalise its imports, as well as exports, so that the two could, through their interaction accelerate the pace of economic development, help raise the standard of living of its citizens and lead to a greater degree of integration with the global economy. This was in complete contrast to strategy of import substitution and export promotion of earlier years.

5.2.5 Strategy of 15 X 15 Matrix

On December 27, 1995, the then commerce minister of the Government of India, Shri P. Chidambaram proposed a new strategy for export marketing on 15 products and 15 country matrix to step up India's export earnings to around US$ 80 billion by 2000A.D, as detailed under Chapter 8. With the change in Government, this strategy too was laid to rest.

5.2.6 Medium Term Export Strategy

During 1997-98, the Commerce Ministry of the Government of India, developed Medium Term Export Strategy, covering sector specific issues, with a view to improve exports to existing and new markets and diversifying the product range.

Product diversification for EU markets would include health products, pharmaceuticals, herbal products and improved marine products. The strategy for N. American markets would involve consolidation of India's position in gems and jewellery and textiles besides engineering chemicals and leather. In East Europe and CIS, efforts to be made to strengthen exports through consignment basis and setting up of warehouses. Asian trade would see increased interaction with ASEAN, negotiation for establishment of SAFTA and widening and deepening of trade with Japan. The export strategy for Africa including West Asia and North Africa would include focus on joint ventures, third country exports and market promotion. Besides, an integrated programme for developing trade with Latin America has been drawn up.

5.3 EXPORT FINANCING AND REFINANCING IN INDIA

5.3.1. Bank Financing

Many countries both developed and developing have devised various schemes for enhancing their export earnings by providing finance to the export sector at relatively lower interest rates at pre-shipment and post shipment stages and covering exports on credit. Our policy framers have recognised the importance of export finance as early as the 1950s by treating exports as priority and setting up institutional machinery, such as Export Risk Insurance Corporation of India 1957 (subsequently Export Credit Guarantee Corporation of India). Export credit (interest subsidy scheme) was introduced in 1968 followed by a refinance window for export through RBI. The commercial banks were directed to open Export Financing cells from the 1970s.

The foundation for the structure of export finance has been built upon various policies relating to the trade, exchange control, credit, international customs practices as well as policy guidelines set by export development agencies like the Exim Bank, financial institutions, Export Promotion Councils and Commodity Boards. Need for finance arises at the Pre-shipment stage (packing credit) in the form of working capital or clean packing credit for procuring, processing, packaging, warehousing and at the post shipment stage. This could be extended against hypothecation of goods or against incentives or receivables.

The post-shipment finance may include negotiation of export bills under documentary credits, purchase or discount of bills against export orders, advance against bills under collection, finance against Government incentives due or undrawn balances. The non fund facilities take the form of Letters of credit for purchase of raw materials or bank guarantees to facilitate exports.

Finance of export transactions has built in extra dimension of risks since it is across national borders and competition extends beyond price, quality and delivery terms and conditions of payment, (including credit terms) and this highlights the importance of availability of credit, its adequacy and its role.

The Government of India appointed several committees such as the G. Sundaram Committee on Export credit in Sept. 1992 and another committee under the chairmanship of Mr. O.P. Sodhani in 1995, to study the entire gamut of foreign exchange and related matters.

The major recommendations of the Sundaram committee were: Export finance should bear interest below 10%, Tax on interest for export credit to be withdrawn, earnings on Export Finance by banks not to be taxed, development of a domestic market for rediscount of export bills, pre-shipment credit to be at internationally competitive prices, working capital limits under Tandon and Chore committees to be raised, limits under consortium lending to be raised to Rs. 10 crores and simplification of procedures for sanctioning of loans by banks.

Some of the recommendations were accepted by Government, but their implementation were less than satisfactory. The interest on export credit was retained at 13% for several years till February 8, 1996 when Banks were permitted to charge discretionary rates for post-shipment credit beyond 90 days. The rate of interest on pre-shipment and post-shipment credit in several countries were less than 10% except in Pakistan and Denmark, while a low 4% in Malaysia. Government has since introduced Pre-shipment credit designated in Foreign Currency(PSC) and Post-shipment Credit

Designated in Foreign Currency(PSCFC) under which credit was available at internationally comparable prices.

5.3.2 Financing by Industrial Development Bank of India

The importance of exports and the need for supporting finance had been recognised since the 1950's. With this view, the Reserve Bank of India introduced during the Export Bill Market Scheme, in respect of bills with a maturity of less than 80 days arising out of export transactions. In 1958, the Refinance Corporation for Industry (RCI) was established. The RCI soon introduced a scheme for refinancing of medium term export credit provided by authorised dealers in foreign exchange, to export bills with a maturity of less than 180 days. The RCI was merged with the IDBI when the latter came into being in 1964. Thus to begin with the IDBI provided only refinance support to the Indian exporters.

Soon after its establishment, the IDBI realised that mere provision of refinance of export credits at a concessional rate was not sufficient to boost exports. Schemes for direct financing of exports, providing a form of buyers and suppliers credit were formulated, in addition extending loans to financial institutions abroad to, facilitate Indian exports. The important role that IDBI plays is due to its position as an apex financial institution in the country and a lender of last resort for exports. With the formation of the Export-Import Bank of India, some of the export support functions of the IDBI have been passed on to the EXIM bank.

5.3.3 Financial Services Provided by the Export-Import Bank of India (Exim Bank)

The EXIM bank was established, under the Export-Import Bank of India Act 1981, to provide financial assistance to exporters and importers and function as the principal organisation for co-ordination of institutions engaged in financing export import trade. The bank has been able to support a range of industry sectors including enterprises set up by professionals and technocrats.

The EXIM Bank promotes Indian exports through a range of programmes like investment loans, loans for export marketing, pre-shipment credit and suppliers' credit for export of products, projects and consultancy. Companies can also avail of facilities such as 'forfaiting' and bulk import finance for import of raw materials and intermediates. EXIM Bank's operations extend to all stages of the business cycle- production, marketing, pre-shipment, overseas investment, import of technology and product development relating to exports.

5.4 EXPORT CREDIT INSURANCE

The Export Credit Guarantee Corporation was set up to extend insurance cover for political and commercial risks as credit is critical to exports to developing countries. The different facilities offered are :

- Standard policies cover credit under 180 days.
- Specific policies cover exports on deferred payment terms including services and construction work as well as turnkey projects.
- Financial guarantees to banks which extend facilities to exporters and special scheme guarantees covering buyers credit, overseas investment insurance and exchange fluctuation insurance.

The equity level of ECGC at Rs. 50 crore is totally inadequate especially in view of joint insurance with institutions like EXIM Bank of USA and is expected to be raised to Rs. 500 crore gradually. The growth in premium earned too presents a dismal picture (Rs. 831 crore in 1957 to Rs.1013 crores in 1995) . By International Standards the equity base should be 1.5 to 2% of risk exposure, which currently stands at Rs. 25,000 crore, calling for raising the equity base to Rs. 375 to Rs. 500 crore. The Corporation has also finalised plans to provide guarantee against the risk involved in exploring new markets.

5.5 EXPORT PROMOTION ZONES AND EXPORT ORIENTED UNITS

It may be recalled that there are seven Export Processing Zones in India, *viz.*, Kandla(Gujarat), Santa Cruz (Bombay), Falta (West Bengal), Noida (U.P.), Cochin (Kerala), Chennai (Tamil Nadu), and Vishakhapatnam (Andhra Pradesh). Among these zones, only Santa Cruz Electronics Export Processing Zone (SEEPZ) is meant exclusively for the export of electronics and gem and jewellery, while the other zones deal with multi-product operations. Export products covered by these zones comprise mainly the groups of electronic and engineering items, chemicals and allied products, textiles, garments, plastics and rubber products.

Exports from all the seven zones totalled Rs. 2653 crore in 1994-95, growing significantly to Rs. 3256 crore in 1995-96 and further to Rs. 4339 crore in 1997-98, having doubled during a short period of time. With improvements in export promotion policies, delegation of powers to field authorities and simplification of customs and excise procedures, the export processing zones are likely to enhance India's export performance.

In the case of Export Oriented Units, it may be emphasised that they enjoy many of the facilities extended to EPZs and have been growing year by year. By the end of 1997, there were 1140 EOUs, being separated from Domestic Tariff Area by means of fiscal barriers.

Exports from all EOUs were of the order of Rs. 4710 crore during 1994-95, increasing to Rs. 7009 crore by 1995-

96. During 1996-97 exports from EOUs stood at Rs. 8715 crore and estimated at Rs.10,500 crore in 1997-98. The combined exports of both EPZs and EOUs were Rs. 13,054 crore and estimated at Rs. 15,309 crore in 1997-98, registering an increase of 17%.

Various incentives have been evolved for further increase in exports. The EXIM-Policy (1997-2002), as well as recent package of facilities for exports, announced by Commerce Minister, Shri Ramakrishna Hegde, offer further incentives to boost exports.

5.6 FOREIGN EXCHANGE FOR TRADE PROMOTION BY EXPORTERS

Export promotion activities undertaken at the firm's level such as travel study tours, market surveys involve expenditure of Foreign Exchange, which is under the purview of The Foreign Exchange Regulation Act 1973 as amended in 1993. After the reforms, exporters are now permitted to deposit 25% of their exchange earnings into Exchange Earners Foreign Currency Account for use in export promotion. Export Oriented Units and units in FTZ, Technology parks and software Technology parks enjoy a higher limit of 50% in EEFC.

The Sodhani committee recommended retention of 100% export earnings in EEFC accounts, allowing financial institutions to deal in Forex just like banks, setting up forex clearing houses and authorising Forex dealers to speculate in cross currency deals.

Against the constant complaint from exporters that interest rates are high, a recent Reserve Bank study (covering 1211 non financial companies and 130 financial companies-Times of India dated 28.1.96 page 1) indicates a decline in interest burden, which has gone down to 32.2% in the second half of 95-96 from 35.4% from the previous period. But a more serious problem evident from a study by Confederation of Indian Industries reported in the Telegraph of Feb. 6, 1996 was paucity of funds available.

Several trade and industry associations(ASSOCHAM, FICCI and Indian Bankers Association) suggest that the Statuary Liquidity Ratio (SLR) and Cash Reserve ratio be further reduced from 28% and 14% respectively (reduced from previous high of 38% and 15%) so as to increase availability of Bank's funds and ease the high call money rates seen recently.

The depreciation of the Rupee against the US Dollar in the Foreign Exchange market, though beneficial to Exporters may lead to increased import bills in terms of rupees.

The Governor of the Reserve Bank, Mr. R. Rangarajan announced on Feb. 7, 1996, following changes in policy and procedures :

- Scrapping of Post Shipment credit designated in Foreign Exchange scheme(PSCFC).
- Freeing interest rate on post shipment export rupee credit over 90 days.
- Hiking interest surcharge on import finance from 15% to 25%.
- Monitoring cancellation of forward contracts of over USD 100,000 by authorised brokers.
- These measures which came into effect on Feb. 8, 1996 are likely to dampen the speculation and has helped stabilise the rupee value *vis-à-vis* the USD.

The immediate fall out of these measures is that export credit beyond 90 days is bound to be more expensive and the small scale sector, which is responsible for about 40% of our exports, is likely to be the hardest hit. According to the Reserve Bank of India once the situation improves they might be rolled back. Whatever the constraints of the Government, the reform of the financial sector has to be reviewed regularly so that our exporters are able to withstand international competition by reduction in interest rates comparable to that prevailing in other countries (suggested in the CII document "Financial Sector Reforms: The unfinished Agenda). Government should also consider enlarging the services to the exporters like Factoring and Forfaiting which await increasing development in India.

A discussion paper by the Department of Economic affairs, Ministry of Finance, Government of India entitled "Economic Reforms, two years after and the task ahead", 1993 suggest a complete ban on generalised loan waivers, phased reduction in SLR and CRR would create an environment for banks to lend to priority sectors. The Economic survey of 1995-96 also recognises the need to bring down interest rates.

Despite the many far reaching measures taken by the Government so far, much is left to be done, especially in the reformation of the banking sector. The Government has to address itself to the macro economic fundamentals like encouraging the saving rate from the current 24% to 30%, removing operational hurdles for companies raising foreign currency outside India and resort to innovative measures like factoring and forfaiting. The Banks should be innovative in raising deposits which could improve credit management system. Availability of credit in sufficient volume with progressive lowering of interest rate would significantly help the cause of export promotion.

5.7 INSTITUTIONAL FRAMEWORK FOR EXPORT IN INDIA

5.7.1 Recent Developments

Right from the Third Five Year Plan period (1966-69), the

Government of India, had been evolving export promotion measures to augment export, develop trade and increase foreign exchange earnings, through changes in import policies and introducing export incentive schemes. Import policies were adapted to be export oriented, so that capital goods, machineries and important inputs could be imported at lower costs for imparting technological improvements to the production base of export oriented industries, which may make Indian goods competitive in world markets. Among such schemes the following are the major ones worth mentioning:

- Export Promotion Capital goods scheme;
- Duty Exemption scheme;
- Export Oriented Units scheme;
- Export Processing Zones scheme;
- Diamond, Gem and Jewellery Export Promotion Scheme;
- Deemed Exports Scheme;
- Export Houses/Trading Houses/Star Trading Houses/ Super Star Trading Houses scheme.

Export Promotion Capital Goods Scheme

Import of Capital goods into India, attracted high import duties. In 1990, the Government introduced a scheme under which duty concession of 25% was granted, subject to export obligation. A second scheme with duty concession of 15% was introduced since 1993. Under the import policy 1997-2002, license holders were permitted to import capital goods at a rate of 10%, with an obligation of exporting four times the cif. value of imports. If the value of capital goods imported was over Rs. 20 crore, the licencees could avail zero duty concession, but with an obligation to export six times the value of imports. In both cases 20% of the value of licences could be utilised to import spares. The EPCG scheme was subsequently extended to computer systems as well as to agricultural and services sectors where the value of imports as well as export obligations were lower.

Duty Exemption Scheme

This scheme was available under two categories—Duty Free Licence and Duty Entitlement Pass Book. The former includes Advance Licence, Advance Intermediate License, and Special Import License, for duty free import of raw materials and other inputs. In the case of Special Import License, manufacturer-exporter could use the facility for import of inputs supplied to the categories recognised as 'deemed exports'. Under the Duty Entitlement Pass Book scheme, import of inputs is permitted against export obligation, and is freely transferable.

Gems and Jewellery

Exporters of Gems and Jewellery are eligible for grant of Replenishment Licences to import of inputs and to replenish their inputs, such as rough diamonds. The licences and the materials imported are transferable after meeting export obligations, within five months from the date of clearance of the imports.

Deemed Exports

These refer to transactions in which the goods supplied are constituent part of exports, and the supplier is paid by the exporter in India. Such 'Deemed Exports' are eligible for a number of benefits including granting of Special Import Licences, Advance Intermediate Licenses, deemed export drawback schemes and refund of terminal excise duty etc.

Export Finance

Availability and cost of export finance determine to a large extent the competitiveness of Indian goods in the international markets. The interest on post shipment Rupee credit has been rationalised since October 1996. Procedures have been laid down by the Reserve Bank of India, to augment export finance by Banks, and the RBI has taken upon itself the monitoring of flow of export credit to the exporters.

Infra-Structure Developments

An inter-ministerial committee has been set up during 1996-97, to oversee development of infra-infra-structure for export trade, which is currently considered inadequate. The IMC had approved 12 proposals for setting up Inland Container Depots and cargo forwarding stations.

Market Development Assistance

Established in 1963 as the Market Development Fund, is now known as Market Development Assistance, support activities like Market Research, Commodity research, areas studies, product promotion and commodity development, export publicity and dissemination of information, participation in trade fairs and exhibitions, trade delegations and study teams, establishment of offices abroad, grants in aid to Export Promotion Councils and similar activities.

Grants in aid are offered to 20 Export Promotion Councils, in additions institutions such as Indian Institute of Foreign Trade, Indian Institute of Packaging, Indian Council of Arbitration and Indian Diamond Institute. As joint ventures abroad offer potential for development, market development assistance is extended to such ventures.

Participation of State Governments

Though a central subject, state governments have increasingly been playing an active role in development of exports. The Indian Institute of Foreign trade had researched export potential of most of the states. The Ministry of Commerce has set up a "states cell" as a nodal agency for interacting with state governments on matters concerning exports, while the state governments have set up Apex level organisations for promoting exports from individual states.

Government Representation Abroad

Commercial wings of Indian Embassies and High Commissions abroad have been strengthened as to respond to enquiries from business abroad and project a favourable image of the country. These commercial wings also help in participation in trade fairs and exhibition in addition to help in settling trade disputes.

Recent Export Assistance Package

Commerce Minister, Shri Ramakrishna Hegde, announced several measures to boost sagging exports, on August 5, 1998, which include following important measures :

- Reduction in interest rates on post-shipment and pre-shipment credit (from 11% to 9%), for the current financial year 1998-99.
- Delayed reimbursement (over 2 months) of duty drawback incentive and terminal excise duties would attract interest from the Government.
- Exporters allowed to furnish legal undertaking instead of Bank guarantee, while going in for duty free import of raw materials.
- Tax holiday facility for EOUs/EPZ extended to 10 years from the earlier five.
- Privately run software technology parks would be included under the Capital Goods Export Promotion Scheme.

- EOUs to be given sub-contracting facilities in the Domestic tariff Area.

These measures are expected to boost sagging exports during the past year.

Recognising the importance of sound institutional framework the Government of India had strengthened the institutional set-up by creation of new and specialised agencies reorganisation of existing ones and enlarging the scope of various organisations. Currently the institutional framework is segmented into seven:

1. Policy formulation body to guide India's trade;
2. Advisory and consultative bodies;
3. Commodity specific organisations;
4. Service Institutions;
5. State Trading Organisations;
6. Export Promotion Agencies at state Govt. levels; and
7. India's Commercial representatives abroad.

5.7.2. Organisational Framework for Export in India

The Ministry of Commerce, as the Apex body is responsible for all policy decisions concerning export promotion. It evolves and directs foreign trade policy and programmes including commercial relations with other countries, state trading, regulations of export-oriented industries, Export Promotion Councils, Public Sector Undertakings, and Free Trade Zones and Export Processing Zones.

Board of Trade

The Board of Trade, reconstituted in 1991, is headed by the Commerce Minister, provides a platform for meaningful dialogue between Government and industry.

The membership is wide enough to include representatives from the Reserve Bank of India, EXIM Bank, and ministries like Finance, Textiles and Industry in addition to the Prime Minister's office. The Presidents of FICCI, ASSOCHAM, CII, FIEO as well as a few area specialists are on the Board.

Export Promotion Board

The relatively poor performance on the export front during 1996-97, prompted the constitution of a new body known as Export Promotion Board (EPB), in 1997, for taking quick remedial action, towards solving problems of exporters and sagging exports. The EPB had taken significant decisions on speeding up clearance of export air cargo, co-ordination among infra-structural agencies and giving priority to sectors like electronics and garments.

Cabinet Committee on Foreign Trade (CCFT)

This high level committee, with the Prime Minister as Chairman, was constituted in July 1998, to review the export performance, deliberate policy issues and introduce measures to accelerate exports. The CCFT along with export promotion board (EPB), a secretary level body, would target major problems faced by exporters.

Director General of Foreign Trade, New Delhi

The DGFT oversees execution of export import policies, through a network of 31 subordinate offices located around the country. The wide network of offices help exporters, especially in export and import licensing.

Director General of Commercial Intelligence and Statistics

The primary responsibility of this agency is collection, compilation and dissemination of Trade information, both inland and foreign. These statistics are indeed helpful for monitoring trade and economic policies, and negotiations of bilateral trade agreements. The Directorate brings out a number of publications in addition to maintaining a commercial library helpful to trade and research scholars.

Export Promotion Councils

The twenty Export Promotion Councils provide both advisory and executive functions to help exporters in different sectors. These are non profit making bodies registered under the Societies Act, and have been assigned the functions as registering authorities under the Import Policy 1998-2002. Their functions include bringing exporters' problems to the notice of the Government, assisting foreign buyers' with information on export capabilities, gathering commercial intelligence through market surveys, delegates reports etc.

Apart from EPCs, there are 7 commodity boards, responsible for production, development and export of commodities such as tea, coffee, rubber, spices, tobacco etc. The Marine Products Export Development Authority (Estd. 1970) and The Agricultural & Processed Food Products Export Development Authority (set up in 1986), carry out similar functions in their respective product sectors. An Export Promotion Forum (EPF) , for the film industry has been set up in July 1988, to promote market for Indian movies, music and audio-visual entertainment products overseas. This organisation is headed by the Secretary, Information and Broadcasting Ministry, Government of India.

Indian Institute of Foreign Trade

Set up in 1964, under the Societies Registration Act, is the premier training and research institution in International Trade. Major activities include training of managers in foreign trade, research into problems facing foreign trade, area and commodity studies and dissemination of information gathered. The Institute offers consultancy services, conducts seminars and holds conferences and workshops on international trade issues.

Indian Institute of Packaging

Since 1966, the Institute has been undertaking research on packing materials, organising training programmes in packaging technology, as well as providing testing facilities for testing and evaluation of packages and packaging materials.

The Export Credit Guarantee Corporation established in 1957, provides export credit insurance and guarantee facilities to exporters and commercial banks. It offers policies protecting exporters from non-payment of proceeds on account of political and commercial risks.

Export Inspection Council

This council offers advice to Government on enforcing quality control and inspection of commodities meant for exports. It arranges pre-shipment inspection as well as process quality control system and some self certification schemes. However recognised Star Trading Houses, Trading Houses and Export Houses and units in EPZs and EOUs have been exempted from the purview of compulsory pre-shipment inspection.

India Trade Promotion Organisation

Consequent to the merger of erstwhile Trade Development Authority and Trade Fair Authority of India, ITPO came into existence from January 1992, as to promote exports and imports through the medium of trade fairs held in India and abroad. It holds buyer seller meets and contact programmes and undertakes publicity through print and electronic media.

Indian Council of Arbitration

Disputes being unavoidable in international trade, the Council was set up to resolve disputes through arbitration, in association with India's commercial representatives abroad, and the International Chamber of Commerce.

Export Processing Zones

Set up as conclaves separated from the domestic tariff area by fiscal barriers, EPZs offer better infrastructural facilities and service support such as customs, and financial institutions. Industries based in EPZs enjoy several fiscal exemptions and an internationally competitive duty free environment.

Export Oriented Units

This scheme was introduced early 1981, and is seen as complimentary to the EPZ scheme. It offers an option in location with reference to raw materials, ports of export, availability of technical skills etc. As on December 1997, 1140 EOUs under the scheme is estimated to have exported a total Rs. 10,500 crore.

Federation of Indian Export Organisations

As an apex body of all export promotion organisations, FIEO has been providing integrated assistance to Government recognised Export Houses, since 1965. It co-ordinates the activities of Export Promotion Councils, Commodity Boards and other agencies with Export Houses in addition to acting as a central co-ordinating agency for consultancy services.

Export Houses and Trading Houses

Export Houses and Trading Houses, recognised by the Government are private businesses helpful in export development. They benefit from financial assistance from the Market Development Agency for approved activities including participation in international trade fairs, sponsorship of trade delegations etc.

Indian International Marketing Centre

As a result of initiative taken by a group of Indian

entrepreneurs with the assistance from the Government of India, the centre was set up in Rotterdam on November 1996, with the objective of promoting export of Indian products, establishing a marketing centre, warehousing facilities and processing activities both in India and abroad, and act as a nodal agency to bring buyers and sellers together.

Public Sector Corporations

The State Trading Corporation and the Minerals and Metals Trading Corporation have effectively been exploring new markets and promoting exports. The STC, set up in 1956, has helped develop trade with centrally planned economies, upgradation of quality of products and mobilise exports from small scale industries. It has been a canalising agency for import of essential inputs. Other subsidiaries of the STC like Projects and Equipment Corporation of India, Tea Trading Corporation, Cashew Corporation of India, and Handicrafts and Handloom Export Corporation have been playing an active role in promotion of exports. The Minerals and Metals Trading Corporation, established in 1963, to promote exports of minerals and metals, have recently taken up activities of a Trading House.

5.8 CRUCIAL BALANCING INVESTMENT SCHEME

As is well known, efficiency of the physical infrastructure in India, is much less efficient than it should be for stepping up country's exports to the desired level. The Government of India introduced the Crucial Balancing Investment Scheme in 1996, to remove impediments to exports with particular emphasis on infrastructure bottlenecks.

The scheme will offer funding support to proposals for removing bottlenecks at ports, roads, airports, export centres and also cover contingency investments not foreseen earlier. The balancing investment under the scheme is not in the nature of a complete project, but an additive or adjunct to an existing facility. During 1997-98 about 18 projects have been approved for various states with a total contribution of Rs. 43.6 crore (against Rs. 20 crore in 1996-97) under the scheme.

5.9 INDIA BRAND EQUITY FUND TRUST

In a major initiative to boost exports on a sustained basis, the Commerce Ministry, Government of India announced on July 11, 1996 the formation of the India Brand Equity Fund (IBEF) Trust, with the major objective of making 'Made in India' label a symbol of quality, competitive price, reliability and customer service. It will sponsor independent studies on Indian products and services in major export markets.

The Trust will also facilitate dissemination of knowledge regarding Indian products and services, obtain feedback on them and sensitize the stakeholders on improvements needed in the products. It will strive to guide the industry associations, semi-commercial organisations and public sector corporations in identifying and pursuing strategies and measures for promoting India's image. Other objectives of the Trust include encouraging interaction among intellectuals, industry, trade (both domestic and foreign) and government in promoting India's brand image. " Creation of country wide awareness of the global imperative of quality and high business ethics will be encouraged" (The Hindustan Times, July 12, 1996).

During 1997-98, this scheme went into operation with an initial budgetary support of Rs. 50 crore and subsequent additional contribution to reach a total of Rs. 99.48 crore. Several exporters, Chambers of Commerce, Export Promotion Councils and Commodity Boards will be acting as facilitators for specific products and countries on a selective basis. These steps under the IBEF is very significant, but it may be sometime before image of India's products is enhanced in overseas markets.

5.10 STATE TRADING

State trading was evolved as an instrument of trade policy during the time of the Great Depression. In the free market economies, state intervention was considered essential to redress many problems including the decline of price and volume of exports of raw materials and foodstuffs, international debt and unemployment confronted by many economies. Foreign trade was the most important element in which government's direct entry played a crucial role. The devices of government regulations and entry barriers consisted primarily of exchange controls, import quota systems and Government monopolies in foreign trade.

The emergence of Soviet Union with complete state monopoly of foreign trade during this period also gave a status to direct intervention of state into foreign trade. According to J.E. Meade, State by monopolising of exports, may limit the quantities to be exported, thus, absorbing the margin between the relatively low home supply price and the relatively high foreign demand price. In this way, state trading monopolies by restricting the volume of imports and exports and by themselves absorbing the monopoly profits can have substantially the same effects in reducing the volume of trade as can be achieved by a system of import or export taxes and licenses. Trade in a way which would result from the payment of import or export subsidies. For instance, a State trading corporation can purchase large quantities from domestic market than a private trader can.

The State Trading Corporation of India has shown very good progress since its inception, achieving a target of Rs. 2836 crore during 1997-98, against Rs. 2525 crore in the previous year. The 12% increase can be attributed to a large extent to higher imports, which is likely to enlarge the basic export production base.

The State Trading corporation and its sister public sector corporations like Minerals and Metals Trading Corporation Metal Scrap Trade corporation and their many subsidiaries are engaged in developing new markets and new products as to accelerate the tempo of export trade.

The international economic situation has been changing very fast and quite significantly during the past few years. The erstwhile USSR is no more : it now the Commonwealth of Independent States. The East European countries are fast shedding their socialistic garb. China has been dynamically adopting market oriented policies under the overall cover of socialism with Chinese characteristics. The theory of countervailing power and days of cold war are over. The present reality is that USA is the only superpower of the world, though China may emerge as an economic superpower in the future when both USA and China may move closer to each other in ideological proximity. The first and the second line tigers of South East Asia had surprised the whole world with their unprecedented growth rates. With the Asian economic downturn since July 1997, they are tigers no more and several governments may be forced to take an active role in international trade.

5.11 CONCLUSION

India has been dynamically revising and reformulating its foreign trade policy. Against this background, export promotion strategies, policies, schemes, incentives and measures adopted so far shall have to be given a new look and perhaps an altogether new model of export promotion strategy shall have to be built for the future in India.

Table 5.1

Organisation of Institutional Framework

Mininstry of Commerce
Government of India

Advisory Body Etc.	*Deptt. of Commerce*	*EPCs CBs & DAs*	*PSUs*	*Other Institutes*	*FTZ/ EPZ*	*Others Important Depts.*
Board of Trade	8 Functional Divisions	EPCs (20*)	STC	EIC	Kandla	DGFT
			MMTC	IIP	SEEPZ	
			PEC	IIFT	Falta	DGCIAS
	1. Admn. & Gen	CBs	TEA Tr.	ICA	Madras	
	2. Finance		Corpn.	IDI	Noida	Custodian
	3. Economic	Tea	Spices	ITPO	Cochin	of enemy
	4. Trade Policy	Coffee	Tr. Corpn.	FIEO	Vizag	Property
	5. Foreign trade	Rubber	ECGC			
		Spices				
COMMITTIEES	Territorial	Tobacco				
EPB	6. Export	Coir				
CCFT	Procucts	DAs				Pay &
	7. Export	APEDA				a/c
	Industries	MPEDA				office
	8. Export Services					

Source : (Ad hoc paper of Prof. S. Ramakrishna of IIFT).

• Including those which are under other Ministries

Note :

CBs	:	Commodity Boards
DAs	:	Development Authorities
EIC	:	Export Inspection Council
EPB	:	Export Promotion Board (Independent one set up in July, 1997)
EPCs	:	Export Promotion Councils
EPZ	:	Export Procession Zone
FIEO	:	Federation of Indian Export Organisations
FTZ	:	Free Trade Zone
ICA	:	Indian Council of Arbitration
IDI	:	Indian Diamond Institute (For trained manpower)
IIFT	:	Indian Institute of Foreign Trade
IIP	:	Indian Institute of Packaging
ITPO	:	Indian Trade Promotion Organisation
PSUs	:	Public Sector Undertakings
APEDA	:	Agri. & Processed Foods Products Export Dev. Authority
MPEDA	:	Marine Products Export Development Authority

Table 5.2

List of subjects Under the Control of Department of Commerce

DEPARTMENT OF COMMERCE (VANIJYA VIBHAG)

I. GENERAL INTERNATIONAL TRADE POLICY

1. International Commercial Policy.
2. International Agencies connected with commercial policy (*e.g.* UNCTAD, ESCAP, ECA, ECLA, EEC, EFTA, GATT, WTO and relating bodies, ITCB).
3. International Commodity Agreements other than agreements relating to Wheat.
4. All matter relating to international trade policy including fariff and non-tariff barriers; preferential trading arrangements; regional trade blocs and economic groupings.
5. All matters relating to anti-dumping investigations and duties taced by the Indian exporters abroad and all work relating to the Designated Authority under the Anit-Dumping provisions of the Customs Tariff Act.

II. FOREIGN TRADE

6. All matters relating to foreign trade including monitoring of trade perfomance, trade negotiations and agreements (including all matters and agreements under General Agreement on Tariffs and Trade/WTO, Commonwealth Tariff Preferences and other preferential trading arrangements *viz.* Bangkok Agreement, SAPTS, GSTP etc.), trade missions and delegations, trade cooperation and promotion and protection of interests of Indian trades abroad.
7. Import and Export Trade Policy and Control excluding the matters relating to :

   (*i*) Import of feature films;

   (*ii*) Export of Indian films - both feature length and shorts; and

   (*iii*) Import and distribution of cine-film (unexposed) and other goods required by the film industry.
8. Directorate General of Foreign Trade.

III. STATE TRADING

9. Policies of State Trading and performance of organisations established for the purpose, including:

   (*i*) State Trading Corporation and its subsidiariese xcluding Handicrafts and Handlooms Export Corporation and Central Cottage Industries Corporation.

   (*ii*) MMTC Limited and its subsidiaries.

IV. TRADING WITH THE ENEMY : ENEMY PROPERTY

10. Trading with the enemy; enemy firms and enemy property reparations (other than German industrial equipment); Controller of Enemy Trading; Controller of Enemy firms; Custodian of Enemy Property for India.
11. International Customs Tariff Bureau including residuary work relating to Tariff Commission.
12. Development and expansion of export production in relation to all commodities, products, manufacturers and semi-manufacturers, and projects including the following:

(a) Agricultural produce within the meaning of the Agricultural produce (Grading and Marking) Act, 1937 (1 of 1937);
(b) Marine products;
(c) Industrial products (engineering goods. chemicals, plastics, leather products etc.);
(d) Fuels, minerals and mineral products;
(e) Specific export oriented products (including plantation crops etc. but excluding jute products and handicrafts which are directy under the charge of this Department);
(f) Consultany, civil construction and tumkey projects.

13. All organisations and institutions connected with the provision of services relating to the export effort including.

(a) Export Credit and Guarantee Corporation.
(b) Export Inspection Council.
(c) Directorate General of Commercial Intelligence and Statistics.
(d) India Trade Promotion Organisation.
(e) Free Trade Zones.
(f) Indian Institute of Foreign Trade.

14. Projects and programmes for stimulating and assisting the export efforts.
15. Production, distribution (for domestic consumption and exports) and development of Plantation crops such as tea, coffee, rubber and cardamom.
16. Processing and distribution for domestic consumption and export of Instant tea and Instant coffee.
17. *(i)* Tea Board
    (ii) Coffee Board
    (iii) Rubber Board
    (iv) Spices Board
    (v) Tobacco Board

Source : Ministry of Commerce.

Table 5.3

Exports Promotion Councils

Product Group	*Controlling Ministry*	*Export Promotion Agency*	*Acronym*	*Main Office At*
1	2	3	4	5
Apparels	MOT	Apparels EPC	AEPC	New Delhi
Basic Chemical etc.	MOC	Basic Chemicals, Pharmaceuticals & Cosmestics EPC	CHEM-EXCIL	Bombay
Constuction Projects	MOC	Overseas Construction Council of India	OCCI	Bombay
Cashew	MOC	Cashew EPC	CEPC	Kochi
Chemicals	MOC	Chemicals & Allied Products EPC	CAPEX CIL	Calcutta
Carpet	MOT	Carpet EPC	CEPC	New Delhi
Cotton Textile	MOT	Cotton Textile EPC	TEXP ROCIL	Bombay
Engineering	MOC	Engineering EPC	EEPC	Calcutta
Electronics	MOC	Eelectronic and Computer Software EPC	ESC	New Delhi
Gems & Jewellery	MOC	Gems & Jewellery EPC	GJEPC	Bombay

(Contd.)

1	2	3	4	5
Handicrafts	MOT	EPC for Handicrafts	EPCH	Bombay
Handlooms	MOT	Handloom EPC	HEPC	Madras
Leather	MOC	Council for Leather EPC	CLE	Madras
Plastics	MOC	Plastics & Linoleums EPC	PLEXICON	Bombay
Powerlooms	MOT	Powerloom Development and EPC	PDEX CIL	Bombay
Rayon etc.	MOT	Synthetic & Rayon Textile EPC	SRT EPC	Bombay
Sports	MOC	Sports Goods EPC	SGEPC	New Delhi
Shellac	MOC	Shellac EPC	SEPC	Calcutta
Silk	MOT	Indian Silk EPC	IS EPC	Bombay
Wool	MOT	Wool & Woollen EPC	WW WPC	New Delhi

* Ever though it is a Federation of Export Organisations for all practical purposes it is treated as EPC under EXIM Policy of India.

MOC - Ministry of Commerce
MOT - Ministry of Textiles
MOI - Ministry of Industry

Source : Annual Reports of concerned Ministries and EXIM Policy April 1997 to March 2002.

Table 5.4

Commodity Boards and Development Authorities

Product Group	*Controlling Ministry*	*Export Promotion Agency*	*Acronym*	*Main Office At*
Agriculture	MOC	Agricultural & Processed Food Products Export Development Authority	APBDA	New Delhi
Coffee	MOC	Coffee Board	CB	Bangalore
Coir	MOI	Coir Board	CB	Kochi
Marine	MOC	Marine Products Export Development Authority	MPEDA	Kochi
Rubber	MOC	Rubber Board	RB	Kottayam
Spices	MOC	Spices Board	SB	Kochi
Tea	MOC	Tea Board	TB	Calcutta
Tobacco	MOC	Tobacco Board	TB	Guntur
General	MOC	Federation of Indian Export Organisations*	FIEO	New Delhi

* Even though it is a Federation of Export Organisations for all practical purposes it is treated as EPC under EXIM Policy of India.

MOC - Ministry of Commerce

MOT - Ministry of Textiles

MOI - Ministry of Industry

Source : Annual Reports of concerned Ministries and EXIM Policy April 1997 to March 2002.

Chapter 6

Liberalisation and Export Promotion

6.1 INTRODUCTION

Increasing numbers of developing countries are unilaterally liberalising trade and during the 1980's, liberalisation seemed to have become contagious in the developing world. In Asia it spread from Taiwan and Korea to Southeast Asia and on to China. In Latin America, it spread from Chile to Mexico and beyond. Recent studies have highlighted this rapid shift towards outward orientation, and have debated both its desirability and sustainability.

Many studies have attempted to assess the impact of trade reform episodes on growth, productivity, fiscal revenues, employment, income distribution, exports, imports and balance of payments. Much debate has resulted, and many issues are still unresolved. As Rodrik (1993) notes, a need for systematic empirical work on the most recent round of liberalisation still exists.

6.2 TRADE LIBERALISATION

The lack of an agreed upon definition of trade liberalisation makes it difficult to assess the extent to which it has occurred. As Greenaway (1992) points out, a more neutral regime can be achieved through a reduction in import barriers, or export subsidies. The latter policy clearly implies an increase in intervention in the trade regime, while the first implies a reduction.

In his 1989 study on this subject, Edwards gives an extensive review of definitions of trade liberalisation. In the major NBER studies by Krueger and Bhagawati, liberalisation meant policy reforms leading to more reliance on the price mechanism, and a reduction in the anti-export bias of the trade regime. Emphasis seemed to be placed on the first part of this definition. Thus, removal of QR's, or a real devaluation which reduced the scarcity premium on QR's constituted liberalisation. The more recent studies by Michaely, Papageourgiou, and Choksi (1991) and Thomas and Nash (1991) appear to include both neutrality and liberality in their definitions of trade liberalisation. Liberalisation encompasses not only a reduction in the anti-export bias of the trade regime, and an increase in reliance the price mechanism, but also a reduction in level of intervention. Inclusion of these concepts in the definition of trade liberalisation means that a large number of policy changes must be considered in an evaluation. Some of these are :

- Lowering average nominal tariffs
- Narrowing the range of nominal and effective tariffs
- A shift from Quantity Restraints to tariffs
- A real devaluation
- A Unification of Multiple Exchange Rates
- Removal of export taxes
- Implementation of subsidies, rebates or compensation schemes

Two World Bank studies argue that countries with overvalued currencies should pursue real devaluation as a first step in the adjustment process. The devaluation must be sustained, and the real exchange rate held stable, for reform to succeed in practice (Thomas and Nash, 1991). But there is still much debate on the inter-relationship between reform of the foreign exchange market, and reduction of trade barriers. Krueger (1986) and Pritchett (1992) discuss the fact that foreign exchange shortages due to overvalued rates and extensive exchange controls may be the binding constraint on a country's trade. Removal of import restrictions without reform of the exchange market would thus be ineffective.

There is general consensus, however, that the success of trade reform will be limited if other domestic distortions are not removed. If domestic financial markets are not reformed (*e.g.* the removal of interest rate ceilings), capital account liberalisation is likely to produce capital flight and dramatic depreciation of the currency—potentially raising adjustment costs. In addition, the tradable sector's response to trade reform may be inhibited. If tax reform does not take place simultaneously with tariff reductions, government revenues may shrink, reducing its ability to finance other programs. These phenomena may increase the political opposition to the reform.

Countries which have been most successful in implementing reform have transformed QRs into tariffs first, and then gradually lowered these tariffs and made them uniform. Direct incentives to exports have not been as important to export growth as real devaluation and import liberalisation. At the same time, exporters' access to imported inputs has been more important for export growth than general export subsidies.

There appear to be strong arguments for transforming QRs into tariffs first, both to remove distortions from rent-seeking and monopoly power, and to increase transparency. This policy would also be revenue increasing, and potentially contribute to the sustainability of the reform. Auctioning quotas might facilitate this transformation by yielding an estimate of the quota premium. Bidders behaviour, however, may lead to higher levels of protection. Only the tariff-quota method appears to transform QRs to tariffs without risking an increase in protection.

If reductions in import barriers are gradual, second-best considerations may support introduction of interim export incentives to offset the remaining anti-export bias. However, these incentives should be reduced concomitantly with import barriers.

6.3 LIBERALISATION IN SOUTH ASIA

In the mid 1980s, all four South Asian countries still protected their import-competing sectors with very high tariffs. Of the four, India and Pakistan had the highest duties. Prior to an increase in 1990, India's basic rates ranged up to 335%. Luxury items in Pakistan faced rates as high as 450%. Although most items faced rates below these, average nominal tariff rates still tended to be quite high.

Bangladesh, Pakistan and India also maintained highly complex and extensive systems of quantitative restrictions, characterised by bans, specific quotas, licensing requirements, and other restraints. These were often in the form of positive lists or negative and restricted lists. The exception was Sri Lanka, which had replaced virtually all quantitative restraints with tariffs in 1977. In 1985, Sri Lanka had no bans, no import quotas, and no domestic content requirements, although a small number of goods still faced licensing requirements.

Significant export controls were maintained in all countries, with the exception of Bangladesh, where only a few commodities were (and still are) affected. By the middle of the decade, however, some export incentive measures (*e.g.*, duty drawback schemes) had been implemented in each country.

During the first half of the 1980s, all four countries were experiencing persistent current account deficits. All but India saw inflation rates above 10% and loss of foreign reserves. Real GDP growth had declined to relatively low levels in Sri Lanka and Bangladesh, but remained fairly high in India and Pakistan (5% and 7% on average respectively). Foreign exchange markets were highly restricted in all four countries. Bangladesh, for example, rationed foreign exchange through its import licensing system, and maintained a dual exchange market.

Some movement toward trade liberalisation took place in the first half of the decade. Bangladesh began replacing QRs with tariffs and reducing the dispersion of tariff rates. Sri Lanka continued its earlier reform by reducing the dispersion in effective rates of protection. Pakistan shifted from a positive list of permissible imports to a negative list. Both Pakistan and India removed some restrictions on imports of capital and intermediate goods, but this most likely raised effective rates of protection in some sectors. As recipients of adjustment loans, all four countries have entered into significant liberalisation programs since 1985, but the approaches have varied.

6.4 LIBERALISATION IN INDIA

The first two five year plans started with optimism and the avowed objectives of growth, self-reliance, reduction of inequalities and alleviating poverty in the country. However even after completing eight Five Year Plans the Indian economy continued to be a low-income one, slow growing and vulnerable to vagaries of climate and political developments. The year 1991-92 was eventful when economic policies started moving in a different direction, and India began significant efforts at trade reform in 1991. Prior to this, high tariffs and severe QRs, coupled with both export controls and export incentives created a wide variance in incentives across industries. Even before an across the board increase in tariffs in 1990, nominal tariffs ranged from 0 to more than 300%, auxiliary duties from 0 to 45%, and countervailing duties from 0 to 50% (World Bank, 1992). In addition, foreign exchange was severely constrained, rationed largely to license holders for imported inputs. Severe balance of payments problems appear to have been a major catalyst in the implementation of the recent trade reform program, as part of an overall stabilisation and adjustment process. Reform efforts have been continual and strong since 1991, with significant changes occurring in 1993.

Among the aims of the reform (World Bank, 1992) were :

- Removing licensing and other Non Tariff Barriers on the import of intermediate and capital goods; removing restrictions on exports and broaden and simplify export incentives.
- Reduce both the level and dispersion of tariffs.
- Simplify and increase the transparency of the trade regime.
- Make the rupee fully convertible.

A radical shift to a floating exchange rate system was brought about. In 1991, the rupee was devalued 20% against the US dollar. By February 1992 an explicit dual exchange market existed, in which most private sector imports (except fertiliser and oil) were purchased at the free market rate. Sixty percent of exporters' earnings could be exchanged at the free market rate. By March of 1993, the foreign exchange market was unified, and the rupee allowed to float. Virtually all current account transactions are now free of controls. Capital account transactions remain subject to prior approval, and capital account convertibility seems long way off.

In recent years about 40% of central government revenues were generated through tariffs, and about one third by tariffs above 110%. During 1996-97, customs revenue was around 34% of gross tax revenue. Despite this, substantial reductions in tariffs have been made since 1991. The maximum tariff has fallen progressively from 350% in 1990-91 to 150% by 1991-92, to 85% in 1993-94 and 50% in 1995-96. Import duties on capital goods dropped from 80% to 30% in 1995-96, and even further for imported capital used by exporting firms. Average tariffs fell between 1990 and 1992 from 128% to 94% in nominal terms, with import-weighted averages falling from 87% to 64%. During 1993 further large cuts were made, lowering the nominal average tariff to 71%, and the import-weighted average to 47%. Dispersion of rates has also been significantly reduced. Further reductions in the levels of and range of tariffs were announced from time to time, as well as a proposal for significant rationalisation of the system in later budgets to the year 1997-98. Finance Minister Shri Yashvant Sinha stated in the Parliament on March 25, 1998, that economic reforms would be deepened, broadened and accelerated in his budget for 1998-99, adding that dynamism to exports will be restored.

Much progress has been made on reducing the extent and complexity of NTBs. In April of 1992, all 26 import licensing lists were abolished, except for a negative list. Goods on the negative list can be imported at market rates if a license is obtained. All items not on this list are now freely importable at market rates. Most intermediate goods and capital goods are not on the negative list and are free of any QR's. However, consumer goods imports remain effectively banned. Estimates suggest that the amount of domestic production covered by NTBs fell from

93% in 1990 to 75% in 1992. This was reduced to less than 50% by 1993.

Despite these reforms, India's average tariffs remain high relative to its competitors, and an extensive amount of domestic production remains protected by NTBs. The fact that intermediate and capital goods have been freed of quantitative restrictions and face lower tariffs suggest that reforms may have increased effective rates of protection, particularly in consumer goods industries.

Prior to reform measures which impeded exports and encouraged exports continued to be introduced simultaneously. For example, in 1988 India increased the number of exported items subject to controls. The following year, duty drawback and cash compensation schemes for exporters were extended. Between March 1990 and March 1993, however, the number of controlled export items fell from 439 to 215. Restrictions on manufactured exports were virtually removed. Over half of the remaining controls are on agricultural exports, however, and many of these are significant impediments. Of the several mechanisms established to encourage exports, the duty exemption scheme and duty drawback scheme affect the largest ports. Improvements have been made in the administration of these programmes, but their effectiveness remains limited by procedural complexity.

6.5 LIBERALISATION—SOME COMMENTS

Several esteemed authors have commented at various times on liberalisation in India and abroad, both from a theoretical point of view as well as from the policy angle. The gist of their comments is related in the following paragraphs.

Export Growth and Export Promotion

Stray evidence correlates trade liberalisation with

appreciable export growth rate and strong growth in the year of liberalisation, more in later years (Michael Michaely, 1991). This growth correlates with depreciation of the real exchange rate. But no correlation between export incentive policies and export growth during or before liberalisation. Evidence emerges of pernicious effort of import restrictions on Export growth and positive impact on the renewal.

Controversy exists among international trade theorists whether sustained outward growth could be achieved through trade liberalisation or incentive neutrality or through selective trade policies that are pro-industrialisation. Strong government guidance of trade policy reform has been recommended, as evidenced from success of E. Asian economies.

An examination of the 1980's performance of developing economies, reveals a higher rate of growth of manufactured goods which was associated with higher economic growth. Those countries which had long term export oriented growth (South Korea, Taiwan) had relied on selective trade and industrialisation policies. Examples of success through purely market oriented policies and incentive neutrality are fewer.

Exports During Trade Liberalisation

Widespread fear is evident that trade liberalisation leads inevitably to the depletion of country's foreign reserves. Twenty seven episodes were studied by Michael Michaely to arrive at following findings. Real Exchange Rate depreciated in 17 out of these 21 episodes showing that strong depreciation of the real exchange rate accelerate export growth. No clear pattern however emerges whether export incentive policies enhance export growth or retard it on the basis of the export growth rate for the period of liberalisation.

Stability of the real rate of exchange is related to long term liberalisation and when the real rate was stable or increased the liberalisation was sustained. Real rate of exchange however is influenced by fiscal and monetary policies and a nominal devaluation seems a necessary condition.

Continuity is needed for export success. A stable exchange rate enables producers and investors to make long term investment plans and are also attractive to exporters planning strategies into the future. Shifting political and economic circumstances affect a durable trade liberalisation policy, which today seems to pose an important challenge to India.

Political stability is a must and implementation of liberalisation even if gradual should not be extended over many years. Six to seven years from the initial launching to something approximating free trade could be considered not too long and would indeed benefit the economy.

Creeping liberalisation, however seems doomed and strong move is needed in the beginning (preferably dismantling quantitative restrictions substantially) not only in intermediate goods but also in consumer goods which do not compete with domestically manufactured products.

Guidelines

Some countries had flirted with liberalisation more than once and most of them were comparatively small. Size plus abundance of natural resources works against liberalisation.

Other factors such as level of development, per capita income and political stability distinguishes liberalisers from non-liberalisers.

Predictability of price (in RE rate) over periods beyond six years of liberalisation (long term policy) was also found conducive to export growth-again in liberalising economy "budget deficit" has been smaller.

Liberalisation has sometimes been launched under stress such as balance of payment deterioration, rapid inflation and slump in production. Motives and goals however varied such as ideological conversion or change in political power, improved resource allocation, accelerated growth, increased exports and reduction in inflation. A subsidiary pressure has been from international bodies like World Bank, IMF and joint multi-country agreements.

Liberalisation launched by a bold step is more successful than one introduced step by step. Radical quality restrictions are conducive to improved liberalisation; The impact of liberalisation on BOP has often been favourable. Any deterioration in BOP has often been due to poor exports rather than increased imports.

Extensive analysis of the impact of trade liberalisation on exports leads to findings that the first year performance of exports are biased whereas the second year shows a stronger impact and the third year manifests an unbiased increase in exports. This has been the experience of India following the reforms of 1991, though recently there has been a slowdown in Exports.

Favourable impact on exports was visible in case of "Strong liberalisation" or where "trade barriers" were high in the pre-liberalisation period. It is the relaxation of the import restrictions and an increase in real rate of exchange which accounts for export expansion. Another view supports a more activist approach since markets work slowly and imperfectly. Therefore, trade liberalisation is to be designed and implemented positively to help in creation of capacity in sectors with comparative advantage. While developing countries moved in earnest, towards trade liberalisation, the developed countries increasingly resorted to selectivity and made use of NTB towards managed imports.

6.6 LIBERALISATION AND FOREIGN TRADE

Export growth rate of 20% per annum in US dollar terms since 1993-94 may not seem particularly accelerating when viewed against import growth. Much of the increase in the unit value of exports has partly been contributed by the interplay of technical factors :

Preponderance of US dollar in India's exports coupled with rupee-dollar stability resulted in rise in rupee as well as dollar estimate of unit value index of India's exports. This inflated overall export growth rates in rupee and dollar terms.

Sceptics have reservations about the 'export-led growth' and consider them unviable and unrealistic. However, they concede the need of export promotion for the overall improvement of the economy but feel that across the board opening of the domestic economy, combined with supply side policies is not sufficient to assure India's balanced foreign trade expansion.

Reform process had produced substantial results but the agenda is incomplete and has a long way to go in terms of making an impact on the living standards of the people. In sum, India is at a crucial junction of the reform process and cannot slacken the direction and magnitude of the reform process.

Three years into the reform program with an average economic growth of 4.9% per annum compared to 2.27% achieved by 30 developing countries, projected India as a future important Asian player in international trade. Euromoney's 'country risk assessment' ranked India from 51 to 45 in a list of 181 countries. Japan EXIM Bank's survey shows India has improved its rating by a big margin from tenth (1994) promising to third in 1995.

6.7 INDIA'S TRADE POLICY - PRE AND POST REFORMS

6.7.1 Pre-Reforms Scenario

Import Trade Control was introduced in India as a war time measure in the early period of the Second World War. In this regard, a notification was issued on May 20, 1940 in exercise of the powers conferred under Defence of India Rules. The main objective of this notification was to conserve foreign exchange resources and to restrict physical imports so as to reduce the pressure on the limited available shipping space. Under the initial order 68 commodities, mainly consumer goods, were brought under control. Subsequently, the import control was extended to other commodities as well. Unprocessed and semi-manufactured steel were brought under control on December 31, 1945.

On February 15, 1945, the import of machine tools was controlled. Many other commodities, particularly capital goods and other industrial requirements came under the purview of import control on September 1946, the Emergency provisions (continuance) Ordinance, 1946 was promulgated to continue import trade control provisions. This was ultimately replaced by the Imports and Exports (Control) Act, 1947 (18 of 1947) which came into operation with effect from 25th March 1947, initially for a period of three years and secondly for five years up to March 31, 1971. Thereafter, the validity of the Act was extended indefinitely. A number of notifications were issued from time to time under the Act which were replaced by a consolidated Order called the Imports (Control) Order No 17/55, dated December 7, 1955. This Order, amended from time to time, continued to be in force.

With a view to making provisions for stringent action for misuse of the import facilities, the Imports and Exports (Control) Amendment Ordinance, 1975 was promulgated on November 4, 1975. The Ordinance was subsequently replaced by the Imports & Exports (Control) Amendment Act, 1976. The Import and Exports (Control) Act, 1947 and the Imports (Control) Order, 1955 as amended from time to time continued. Similarly, the Exports (Control) Order was also issued under Section 3 of the Imports & Exports (Control) Act, 1947 from time to time.

After attaining Independence, India followed an import substitution and self-reliance oriented strategy for its economic development. The import-export policies were issued on year to year basis, which were subsequently replaced by a three year import-export Policy in 1985 with a view to providing continuity and stability to the Trade regime. Of the three 3-year Import-export policies issued during 1985-86 to 1991-92, the first 3 year Trade policy (1958-88) could complete is full tenure. The subsequent two 3 year policies were cut short by one so as to make further improvements in the Exim Policy.

Import Controls were relaxed to a very limited extent by placing some items on the OGL list of imports. However in 1976-77 the duty free licensing scheme was for the first time introduced with a view to facilitating export production. Over the period, the OGL list was also substantially enlarged.

The technological gap evident in capital goods sector and the structural changes which took place since the early fifties and the mid seventies, necessitated re-examination of the import-export Policy. The Government of India appointed three committees one after the other in this regard:

1. The Alexander Committee (1978) recommended that the Indian industry may be opened up to

international competition with a view to improving the productivity of its capital and labour and upgrading the quality of its products. The sweeping liberalisation recommended was not given effect and the liberalisation of imports followed on selective basis.

2. The Tandon Committee was appointed in 1980 with a clear focus on export strategy. The Committee noted the adverse effect of protecting the domestic industry by way of customs tariffs, licences and quantitative restrictions on imports on the overall export business.
3. The Tandon committee was followed by the Abid Hussain Committee in 1985. Most of the recommendations of the Committee were accepted and in the consequence the first 3-year import-export Policy (1985-88) was introduced. Many crucial raw materials and capital goods were placed on the OGL list and quantitative restrictions and tariffs were also somewhat reduced. However, considerable protection to the domestic industry still continued.

6.7.2 Restrictions on Import of Capital Goods

153 items of capital goods, plants, machinery and equipment were banned for import. About 1400 items of machinery and equipment for the various sectors of the economy were permitted for import on OGL to the eligible actual users in 1991 as against 79 items of capital goods in 1976-77.

All other items of capital goods were allowed for imports against a license subject to essentiality certificate from the DGTD/Director of Industries, indigenous clearance through advertisement procedure and approval by the Capital Goods Committee. Import of capital goods for sectors such as fertilisers, basic drugs, power generations etc. was permitted on a global tendering basis.

As regards import of second-hand capital goods, all the 1400 specified items of machinery and equipment which were on OGL, were allowed for import against license subject to essentiality certificate from DGTD/ Director of industries, indigenous clearance through advertisement procedure and approval by the Capital Goods Committee. All other second-hand capital goods were not permitted for import.

6.7.3 Restrictions on Import of Production Inputs

Over 900 items of production inputs were allowed for import on OGL subject to actual user condition and other specified conditions. The rest of the production inputs *viz.* raw materials, components, intermediates etc. were imported subject to certain specified conditions through various categories of licenses, Exim Scrips, additional replenishment licenses. Additional licenses were also used for import of restricted production inputs. The import was sought to be made only to bridge the gap between demand and supply keeping in view the foreign exchange resources position.

Besides the production inputs, about 800 items of gems and jewellery equipment, life saving equipment, drugs, crude drugs, dental equipment, surgical sutures and needles, ophthalmic equipment and diving equipment were importable on OGL basis subject to actual user condition. About 75 items were also placed on OGL list for stock and sale. As against 97 items of production inputs on the OGL list in 1982-83, the number expanded to over 900 items in 1991-92.

6.7.4 Canalised Items

In all 53 items were under canalisation of which 43 items comprised raw materials and 10 other specified items such as petroleum products, drugs, fertilisers etc.

6.7.5 Administrative Measures

In order to avoid any default in its international obligations, the Reserve Bank of India resorted to administrative measures in November 1990 to further restrict imports by increasing the cash margin requirements and cost of import finance on the one hand and limiting the access to bank credits for imports on the other. The RBI restrictions with some relaxation in March 1991 for the export sector continued in 1991-92. In consequence of these restrictions the number of licenses issued in 1991-92, as per the provisional licensing data available with DGFT, came down to 97,250 against 1,14,553 in the preceding year, registering a decline of 15%.

6.7.6 Notified Input Output Norms

In April 1990-91 when the 3 year trade policy (1990-93) came into operation only 571 input-output norms for the Duty Exemption Scheme were notified, which is also indicative of the fate of the scheme, as against over 4800 as of today.

6.7.7 Export Incentives

As an instrument of export promotion, incentives in terms of replenishment licenses, Special Replenishment licenses, Exim Scripps, Additional licenses, Cash Compensatory Support, and Duty Drawback were used. Export Promotion Schemes such as Export Promotion Capital Goods Scheme at 25% Customs Duty, International Price Reimbursement Scheme (IPRS) were also introduced from time to time.

6.7.8 High Customs Tariff

High Customs Tariff rates were also used to restrict imports and the peak rate was kept well over 300%.

6.7.9 Post Reforms Scenario

The process of liberalisation started in July 1991 with the objective of developing an environment conducive for generating a fair and free competition among different agents of production and distribution of goods and services, of finance and trade, both public and private, domestic and foreign, small and large alike. The first two sectors which witnessed reforms were the trade policy and the industrial licensing. The trade policy witnessed changes on 4th July and 13th August 1991 followed by the liberalised export-import Policy (1992-97), so as to make it co-terminus with the Eighth Five Year Plan. The new Industrial Policy which was announced in the Parliament on July 24, 1991, dispensed with the formal licensing requirements for almost all the industries excepting a few owing to the special considerations of sensitivity and environment safety.

The old legal regime governing the country's foreign trade *viz.* import-export (Control) Act, 1947, Import (Control) Order, 1955 and Export (Control) Order, 1988 was replaced by the Foreign Trade (Development & Regulation) Act, 1992, Foreign Trade (Regulation) Rules, 1993 and the Foreign Trade (Exemptions from application of Rules in certain cases) Order, 1993. With the advent of new legal regime and the issue of the export-import Policy (1992-97), the era of restricted trade regime witnessed its demise.

The Exim Scrips at a uniform rate of 30% on almost all export products replaced the Replenishment licenses on August 13, 1995. The Rupee witnessed its devaluation first on 1 July followed by 3 July 1991 ranging between 18 to 20% against the major world currencies and was made partially convertible in the 1992-93 budget. The Exim Scrip and the Cash Compensatory Support (C.C.S) witnessed their demise with the advent of partial convertibility. The partial convertibility of Rupee permitted the exporters to get their export proceeds to the extent of 50% converted into Rupee at the market rate and the balance 40% at the official rate. They were also allowed to retain 15% of their export proceeds in foreign currency in their Export Earners Foreign Currency Account (EEFC). The EOU/EPZ units were allowed to convert their entire export proceeds at the market rate.

Full convertibility of the Rupee was introduced through the 1993-94 budget and thereby the total export proceeds were made convertible at the market rate. The exporters are also permitted to retain 25% of their export proceeds in foreign currency in their EEFC accounts. However, the EOU/EPZ units may retain 50% of their export proceeds in their EEFC account.

6.7.10 Freedom for Import

The Exim Policy (1992-97) which came into operation with effect from April 1, 1992 has provided full freedom for import of Capital goods and production inputs which were hither to under restricted trade regime, with the exception of much pruned negative list of Import and Export items which are banned, restricted or canalised for import on ground of socio-religious, safety, security, environment, international conventions and the like.

6.7.11 Import of Capital Goods and Production Inputs

All the new capital goods required for use in manufacturing, mining, agriculture, aquaculture, animal husbandry, floriculture, horticulture, pisciculture, poultry, sericulture and the services sector are placed on OGL for stock and sale. The import of second hand capital goods which was permitted only in 19 specific sectors free of licensing procedures until 1993-94 was subsequently allowed in all the sectors. The condition of 7 year age was also dispensed with. However, the condition of 5 year residual life and the actual user condition continues.

All the raw materials, components, intermediates, spares, parts etc. are freely permitted for import even for stock and sale purposes. In addition, the second-hand goods in the form of waste, scrap, seconds and defectives except hazardous or toxic waste subject to certain specified conditions; waste paper, used rubber tyres with one cut in bead wire and used rubber tubes into two pieces; woollen rags/synthetic rags/shoddy wool in completely mutilated form and PET bottle waste/scrap, were allowed.

6.7.12 Import Licenses

There is not *'per se'* licensing regime in the current Exim Policy. Whatever, licenses are issued under the trade policy, they are primarily related to augmenting exports. Under the Export Promotion Capital Goods Scheme, two types of licenses are issued. Where the license value is Rs. 20 crores and the license at concessional Custom Duty of 15% may be issued. These licenses are subject to specified export obligations. The EPCG Scheme which was introduced in 1990-91 at 25% concessional Custom Duty, is now available duty free or Concessional Custom Duty of 15% as indicated above.

The second Scheme under which the duty free licenses are issued is the Duty Exemption Scheme. This Scheme is meant for providing all the production inputs both on OGL and negative list, having nexus with the export product at international prices for export production. The licenses are issued with a specified value addition and export obligation.

The third important Scheme is the Passbook Scheme. Under the Scheme, the exports are made first and in case the specified value addition is attained, the basic customs duty leviable on the imported inputs deemed to have been used in the export product as per notified input-output norms, is calculated for giving credit in the Passbook. Such credit is used for debiting the basic and additional customs duty leviable on OGL, sensitive list and the special import license shopping list items if imported subsequently by the Passbook holder, even for stock and sale.

As an incentive, special Import Licenses are granted to all categories of export houses at specified rates. This license is also granted to the quality certificate holders under IS 9000 (series) or BIS 14000 (series). EOU/EPZ units acquiring ISO 9000 (series or IS/ISO 900 series quality classification are also now made eligible for SIL. In the current year (1995-96), the export of electronic goods, telecommunication equipment and services are also made eligible for Special Import Licenses (SIL) at specified rates. Deemed exports are also eligible for SIL at the rate of 6% of the FOR value (excluding all taxes and levies). The Special Import Licenses are transferable and valid for import of specified items of negative list including consumer goods, as given in the shopping list of SIL.

6.7.13 Customs Tariff Rates

The customs tariff rates are continuously on the decline since 1991. In July 1991, the peak tariff rate was brought down to 150% from over 300%. It was further slashed to 110% in 1992-93, 85% in 1993-94, 65% in 1994-95 and 50% in 1995-96. At present, the minimum rate is 35% and maximum 50%. The Central Excise rates have also witnessed downward reduction and more items are brought under the MODVAT net.

6.8 CONCLUSION

To recapitulate, the process of liberalisation introduced in India had attracted immense interest from concerned parties around the world. It is of grave concern to them whether India continues its process of liberalisation. This would call for political stability in India and frank statement in clear terms by all the political parties of the country that liberalisation shall be pursued in the future irrespective of the political party that is in power in India. Again, it is perhaps rightly said that to be meaningful and effective, liberalisation should be completed within a period of six years or else if the pace is too slow stretching over a decade, liberalisation may not yield the desired results.

Chapter 7

Export Promotion Strategies in India—Some Suggestions

7.1 INTRODUCTION

Perusal of the six preceding chapters would reveal that India has been making serious efforts to evolve suitable measures for enhancing its export capability. However, the achievements have been far below our needs and expectations. This is leading to a crisis scenario. Hence it is necessary to examine afresh all our export promotion endeavours so as to find out what is wrong with our policies and efforts and to redesign the export promotion endeavours. In this chapter, an attempt has been made to examine at the grass root level and at the national level, the various export promotion policies, schemes, incentive and measures in their operations and suggestions have been formulated for their suitable change in the future.

7.2 COMMENTS ON CURRENT EXPORT STRATEGIES

Production

India's exprot effort hitherto emphasised small scale sector (responsible for about 40% of India's exports) but the anticipated export growth of 15-20% can only be achieved through higher production from medium and large sectors which are capable of ecomomies of scale. Manufacturers/ exporters should plan production purely for exports rather than rely on exportable surplus after domestic market consumption. Larger units should receive incentives only on their exports.

Hi tech Export Parks offer a single window clearance of all state and central government approvals of services of customs, commodity inspection, taxation, banks, insurance, export transportation, post office, telecom, department of electricity/water, gas etc. along with hotels and restaurants. In fact it is a small export township.

The export processing zones enjoy reduction or exemption from enterprise income tax and the consolidated industrial and commercial tax, licences, non application of pollution control guidelines, etc. similar to the Maquillodoras of Mexico.

Export Technology Park schemes could be developed around small ports like Pondicherry, Goa as well as Andaman and Nicobar Islands, where FDI is accorded special treatment and incentives (tax holidays) and liberal labour laws and exit regulations apply. An atmosphere of unique export culture can be built around these parks. State governments have to be actively involved in these developments, especially the centrally administered areas like Pondicherry and Andamans.

According to Pankaj Ghemahat, Professor of Business, Harvard Business School, Indian products are very costly and highly priced to create an explosion in the domestic market. And they are too low in quality to make a big dent in the export market.

Quality

India's major export markets are the developed countries, which demand a high quality of products. The international image of Indian products is none too high and an intensive effort to inculcate quality consciousness among exporters is to be encouraged, assistance to gain ISO 9000 certification scheme offered and state governments need to support quality consciousness by enlarging testing facilities.

Technology

To keep up with technological developments around the world, increased outlay for R&D is called for; as in other developing countries like Brazil and China. Special incentives such as tax exemptions on R&D expenditure, need to be introduced.

Intermediate Goods

Export growth in manufactures such as garments, leather and diamonds is due mostly to original equipment manufacture as per customer's brands. Establishing Indian brands in the international market is a long arduous and expensive process. The first step should be to focus on intermediate products for world class manufacturers.

Export Consortia

Smaller exporters should be encouraged to form "Export Consortia' to enter new markets, and execute large orders from existing markets, without compromising the identity of individual exporters. Again vertical association of suppliers of components and manufactured finished products could ideally form export consortia in specific product segments wherein each partner is committed to the success of the final product. With changing consumer preferences around the world, designs gain added importance. New products and new designs for the export markets need to be encouraged and successful designs awarded recognition.

Niryat Bhavans

The Assocham have recommended establishment of 'Niryat Bhavans'—exclusive centres for export promotion, housing offices of all export councils, Federation of Indian Export Organisation with conference facilities, as well as centres of trade information and database where overseas buyers could pay one visit to gain information on exports. Such centres may be set up in major cities like Delhi, Bombay and Madras.

Role of Export Houses

Export houses have been developed since 1960, as specialised marketing institutions for promoting exports of a range of manufactured consumer and industrial products. This was followed by a category of Trading Houses in 1981, and Star Trading Houses with progressively higher threshold limits of export performance. Federation of Indian Export Organisation was set up as a model agency for registration of export houses.

A sophisticated and highly competitive international market, demands professionalism in marketing. The Sogo Soshas of Japan and Chaebols of South Korea have been highly successful conglomerates. The facilities extended to export houses in the form of Market Development Assistance grants, special import licensing schemes, advanced licensing schemes and export promotion capital goods scheme have to be made more generous.

Market development assistance for FIEO such as sales cum study tours, participation in fairs and exhibitions, advertising in foreign media, production of publication, activities such as market surveys and feasibility studies are funded by the Ministry of Commerce. MDA grants however seem to be less than adequate and may call for selective enhancement.

Large industrial houses should be encouraged to establish an export division whose central activity is exports and joint venture industries with foreign industrialists, for exports.

Agricultural Exports

Starting as an exporter of agricultural products and raw materials, India since 1947 had no deliberate strategy for exports from this important sector. This seems ironic as the government had based its domestic policy in favour of agriculture and farm labourers. The farm lobby exerted less pressure and agriculture ministry seemed to rely on conservative strategy of retaining procurement prices and subsidies. Since 1991, it is the industry which enjoyed the benefits of market reform.

Agriculture's contribution to the country's exports has come down from 30.65% in 1980-81 to 17.61% in 1992-93—but net foreign exchange earned has increased significantly from Rs. 2057 crores to Rs. 3766 crores over the same period, at constant 1980-81 prices. During the four years 1988-89 to 1992-93, value of agricultural exports grew by 71% from Rs. 2198 crores to Rs. 2766 crores. Ashok Gulati *et al.* in 'Export Competitiveness of Select Agricultural Commodities' observe that the agricultural export has diversified from tea, coffee and tobacco to marine products, cereals, fruits and vegetables and their processed forms. During 1996-97, value of agricultural and alied exports were Rs. 23988 crores as against Rs. 20,442 crores in 1995-96.

Among the constraints faced by the agricultural sector were NTB like quota, canalisation and minimum export prices, in addition to an overvalued exchange rate till 1991. The potential for agricultural exports continue to be good as India is the second largest producer of rice and fifth largest producer of wheat though exports constitute only 1% of total production. India's share of production in fruits is second after Brazil (8 % of world produce) and follows China in production of vegetables (12% of world produce). Yet India's share of world exports is less than 1% of commercial production of both vegetables and fruits.

A strategy to increase agricultural exports has to take into account the low productivity of crops like rice, wheat and fruits and vegetables, lack of commercialisation, due restriction on corporations to own land as well as shift in demand towards dairy products, eggs and meat, due increasing income and changing lifestyles. This could release more farm products for export. Nominal production coefficient is useful in determining crop competitiveness based on current levels of technology and infrastructure. If the estimate of divergence between the domestic price and the international price after accounting for transportation and marketing costs is less than unity then the commodity is likely to be competitive in the export market. Based on NPC, competitiveness of rice is 0.46 which means that Indian price of rice is 54% lower than international prices while wheat has a score of 0.86, meaning wheat prices are 14% lower than international prices. Fruits such as mangoes, grapes, bananas, sapotas, apples and lychees enjoy absolute competitive advantage. Vegetables like onions, potatoes and tomatoes also enjoy competitive advantages. These subsections however, suffer from problems of storage, transportation and marketing facilities.

To exploit the potential of the agricultural sector, several reforms are called for such as fast track facilities for transport, quality control, banking, storage at air/sea ports, abolition of cold storage order (under Essential Commodities Act). Research and development to better yields and policy to encourage investment are necessary. Land ceiling acts have been the biggest hurdle in developing commercial farming.

Cashew exports emerged as the largest of Indian agro-exports to over 50 countries including USA, Japan, Russia, UK, Hong Kong and Germany.

Manpower Exports

With the third largest reservoir of skilled manpower in the world, receipts of $2.7 billion from inward remittances is considered low compared to Philippines, Thailand, and Sri Lanka. A more liberalised, less bureaucratic and transparent manpower policy is called for.

Developed nations have reservations about importing manpower from India because of the danger of permanent immigration. It has been suggested by the FICCI that issuance of temporary passports be considered to allay such fears. Extensions of passports to follow subsequent contract of employment may be made by the Indian missions abroad.

Export of Services

Exports of services are limited to select areas like banking (to service the Indian community) and hotels. India should attempt to develop, albeit in a modest way, internationalising of such service industries to gain from technological, managerial and low cost skill of its populace.

Consultancy exports in infrastructure projects have recorded steady progress, and were Rs. 110 crores in 1987-88. The Exim Bank could extend 10% assistance, as well as facilities against overseas credits tied up with consultancy contracts. This sector could also extended for Income Tax exemption on foreign exchange earned abroad, and special status akin to Export Houses and Star Trading Houses.

Project Exports

Exports of projects from India had an uneven record of performance. Potential in ASEAN Countries has to be tapped. The exports suffer from inadequate financial support, in addition to problems of bureaucratic hurdles and procedural delays. During 1997-98(April to Dec.), value of contracts secured was Rs. 1671 crores, registering a substantial increase of about 40% over the preceding year. This is attributed to high value contracts secured from Saudi Arabia, Syria, UAE and Indonesia.

Deemed Exports

Need encouragement by freeing all indigenous inputs used in Exports from excise duty and sales tax as they do help in reducing import bills .

Need for dissemination of information relating to export cannot be overemphasised. Such data on markets should be available at one point such as National Informatics Centre (NIC) and Chambers of Commerce like Assocham, FICCI, Export Promotion Councils etc. They should cooperate in providing relevant data to the centre.

State Governments

A deeper involvement of states in Export Promotion is to be aimed at, since exporters are operating mostly in the states and need the support of the state governments in several areas of their business. To motivate the State governments, the FICCI had suggested that 5% of foreign exchange earned by the state be allocated to the state development for promoting exports. Often, as in the case of Kerala, state governments complain that foreign exchange earned by the state is hardly invested in the state, forcing the state government to increase local taxes (sales tax, octroi etc.) which impedes the growth of exports. A separate cell to assist exporters within each state, would be a welcome step. All inputs that go into exports are to be exempted from local taxes. Setting up of "Niryat Bhavan" in state capitals would publicise the state's endeavour in the field of export.

Export Culture

Almost all of the successful Newly Industrialised

Countries of East Asia, had generated growth in exports through imbibing export culture from the highest echelon of the government to the factory floor. Years of "National fervour" following Independence and "Import Substitution Philosophy" and accepting the socialistic model of state enterprise had relegated the concept of interdependency of economies around the world. Today, no nation can insulate itself from the world economy, if it has to provide a high standard of living for its citizens. A negative and anachronistic attitude towards exports has to be dispelled at each and every level if India has to play the important role in world economic growth it deserves.

Regular training, at all levels of government and industry on the role and significance of export in a large economy such as ours has to be organised. Government and industry publicity machine has to be geared to bring this message to the people at large.

Export related departments like customs, Central Excise, Banks, Transport in fact all institutions having any relation with export activities are to be exposed to programmes which give them an overall picture of the export process and the contribution of each of the departments to export growth. This would help co-ordination and more efficient interaction between units engaged in exports.

Role of exports in the nation's economy, is to be included in all business studies. Further research and training institutes, such as IIFT, are to be set up in various parts of the country more like the IIT, specialising in export. This would lead to a number of specialists in Foreign Trade, who could bring professionalism into this important area of economy.

India Awareness Year

Just as we organise tourism year, India awareness year

are to be organised, to project the India label both at home and abroad. The way ahead could be arduous and risky, but with concerted effort from the central and state governments as well as the industries, India, could achieve what many others have done before. Any delay, could make the task more and more difficult.

Power

The industrial sector, which is the major consumer of energy, suffers from severe shortage of power—with a peak shortage of 18% —is immediately to be relieved by power projects around the country.

Shipping

Major areas needing attention are poor tonnage, modernisation of fleets, diversification of fleets and avoidance of delays in shipping . Charges are one of the highest in the world. The number of ships plying in coastal and overseas trade is only 418½ with GRT 6.03.

Ports

Existing capacities are inadequate and need expansion , modernisation and improvement in efficiency. Smaller ports could be developed jointly with other countries. Development of private ports to be given some priority as power sector and treated as industry. Tax holidays applicable to EOU's to be extended to private ports.

Airports and Civil Aviation

Upgradation of airport infrastructure is urgently needed in addition to :

- Better handling facilities
- Augmentation of uplift capacity of cargo
- Improvement of Civil aviation is linked with development of tourism, which is another foreign exchange earner

Export Oriented Units (EOU) and Export Processing Zones (EPZ)

India was first among developing countries in establishing EPZ in 1966, though the record has been very poor—exports of Rs.1200 crores—against an investment of Rs. 400 crores is much below what was expected.

Convertibility of current and capital accounts would be attraction for exporters both Indian and foreign. Since convertibility on capital accounts for the whole of the country could take some time, it could initially be extended to units operating in the EPZ/EOU. This could help these units bring in foreign currency and repatriate profits.

EOU and EPZ could be allowed to freely import items for exports of manufactured items, as well as trading and services. The units will be free to undertake market development expenditure. A national EPZ/EOU authority could be created to administer genuine single window clearance and full convertibility system.

Indian Direct Investment Abroad

Investment below two million dollars is subject to automatic approval and the limit is seen as too low. When Indian share in foreign investment is through machinery, equipment and know-how, the limit is $500,000 again which is considered low. Joint ventures, subsidiaries, and equity in established companies may help Indian exporters gain entry in developed markets.

Specific Policies

(a) Rate of Interest. Rupee finance for exports should be made easier and rate of interest to be brought down to 10%, still 2-3% higher than LIBOR, and interest in other exporting countries. Pre-shipment finance, for dollar credit and post shipment finance could be clubbed together into a single facility at a competitive rate.

(b) Special Import License. The limited number of items covered under the scheme reduces the benefit of SIL. It should be more broad based by including items like newspapers, petroleum, furnace oil, seeds, edible oils, fatty acids, raw silk, cereals etc.

(c) Exports of Value Added Products. India needs to export more branded products and establish a market for Indian brand names. Sales promotion activities to be supported by release of foreign exchange by RBI. Exchange Earners Foreign Currency Account limits the usage to 24 items, and in selected currencies. The EEFC account has to be made more flexible and adaptive to be of real benefit to exporters.

(d) EPCG Schemes. Capital goods scheme, to induce reduction in customs duty in line with the reduction in tariff of capital goods (55-35%).The EPCG scheme has since been extended to supporting manufacturers and intermediate manufacturers operating under the advance licensing scheme (backed by disclaimer from the ultimate exporter).

Fiscal support to exporters under section 80 HHC, is ineffective in those cases where the exporter also deals in the domestic market in products with a high import content. He has to incur high sales tax and excise duty and is also denied the export incentive.

Under section 80HHB exporters are presently given 50% exemption on export related income in convertible foreign exchange. These are potential areas and should be given 100% exemption. Dividends from joint ventures and overseas subsidiaries remitted in foreign currencies should be categorised along with earnings from export and made tax free. This should be applied to exchange earned from technical and marketing fee or agency commission earned in foreign currency.

The Role of the Corporate Sector

The large corporations and industrial houses are to give a lead to the export growth, as they alone have the capital, managerial know-how and international links needed. In this Indian corporations have to follow the example of 'Sogo Soshas' of Japan and 'Chaebols' of South Korea. The success of the above conglomerates is partly attributable to special status accorded to them by their governments.

In a protected market as in the past, the industrial houses primarily targeted the domestic market. But with increasing competition in the domestic front, the value of liberalisation, the larger houses would be more than willing to look at opportunities abroad.

The corporate big wigs should be encouraged to :

- Make exports as part of their corporate mission and set industry specific targets.
- Improve productivity through technology upgrade without losing site of quality.
- Market aggressively in select areas.
- Help develop a good image for Indian products.
- Better business relations and practices through reliability in dealings.
- Conform to specifications, adhering to delivery schedules.
- Adhere to internationally acceptable trade practices.

In these, the government should actively participate in discussions with business associations like FICCI and Assocham to understand each others problems and in establishing a better export culture among businessmen.

Strategic Steps

The Government of India should try to strengthen trade

relations with other countries, perhaps leaving political considerations aside. Often in the past, our trade has been influenced by different political factors *e.g.* our relationship with Israel, South Africa, Vietnam, Cuba etc. India had lost a lucrative market in Africa, in the post Independence era by ignoring these markets. Similarly, India has to make use of the growing economies of South East Asia by attracting them to invest in infrastructure projects, by encouraging joint ventures and investments in markets which have Indian presence. Similarly, the establishment of SAPTA, would help India more than other members.

A more flexible and encouraging environment to be made available for Indian investment abroad. The approval system has to be made less cumbersome and less bureaucratic in approval procedures.

Factoring

Defined as "a finance house (or bank) called the factor, agrees to relieve the exporter from the financial burden of the export transaction, in particular, the collection of price due from the overseas buyer, so that the exporter can concentrate on his real business, the selling and marketing of its products". The factor who purchases the book debts or receivables also provides related services such as administration of client's sales ledger, provision of pre-payment against debts purchased (upto 80%), collection of debts and covering the risk involved.

Since 1991, the State Bank of India has set up a new subsidiary SBI Factors and Commercial Services Pvt. Ltd. (SBI Factors) to serve industrial and commercial units in various industries like textiles, plastics, packaging, oil extracts, printing ink, chemicals, fertilisers and consumer durables.

Factoring will have a stabilising influence on trade

and would facilitate judicious credit control, efficient sales ledger administration and expeditious debt collection, especially for small and medium sized companies with limited access to capital markets. Factoring further assists the exporter in multiplying his turnover which otherwise may be held up for want of funds. Indian exporters would indeed benefit by development of factoring in future.

Sectoral Perspectives

India's relative strength and weaknesses in selected sectors need close scrutiny for identifying future prospects. Some sectors while established for several decades, need nurturing back to health as to gain acceptability in the international markets. A few of the selected sectors are discussed in the following pages. They are consumer goods, agriculture products, technology exports, turnkey project exports, direct investment abroad, service exports, oil seeds, garments, diamonds and gold jewellery.

Consumer Goods

Manmohan Singh at the "Global Conference of Indian Trade and Investment" organised by All India Association of Industries observed that "India's consumer goods industry has a good future, but has to shed its fear of foreign competition. The consumer goods industry has to be gradually opened to foreign investment so that India's capacity to export consumer goods is enhanced."

India cannot say that she will not import certain goods, while exporting everything India has to integrate with the global markets sooner rather than later and quality will be the key criterion. The unprecedented integration of the global economy poses opportunities as well as dangers.

Technology Exports

Technology exports would consist of capital goods, metal

manufactures, machinery and instruments, transport equipment and industrial plants. They have recorded a substantial increase in exports totalling US$ 7030 million during 95-96.

Frankena (1973-74) had focused on design deficiencies in Indian engineering exports and lack of design research and development work. India could benefit from improved technological capability. Role of multinationals in Indian exports of technological products is minimal. The only way to enter export markets is to identify components/parts which can be subcontracted by Indian manufacturers. Exports of engineering goods from select developing countries show that countries like Argentina, Brazil, Hong Kong, South Korea and Singapore enjoy higher share of world exports. The competition from East European countries with financial and technical support from West European companies is also likely to be severe in future.

Various licensing monopoly control and small industry promotion policies held back the growth of large firms which alone had the capability to export technological products. Various supply shortages (power, steel), transport bottlenecks and labour problems contributed in limiting attack on foreign markets.

Engineering products are the growth items of the future though India today accounts for hardly 0.2% of world trade. In components, parts, accessories, hand tools and certain machine tools, two-wheelers, durable consumer goods like sewing machines, electric fans, EPNS wares, steel wire products, etc., India holds promise. According to engineering export promotion council (EEPC), India's export of engineering goods and services has touched US$ 3766 million during 1995-96.

Turnkey Plant Exports

Many of the developing countries without a domestic

capital goods base and associated engineering skills, rely on imports of entire plants. This helps individual manufacturers to cooperate with several different enterprises (producers, engineering consultants, process technology owners and civil contractors). Indian companies would do well in undertaking detailed engineering project supervision and other labour intensive (rather than technology intensive) parts of turnkey jobs along with developed country enterprises who are strong technologically.

The major technological content may have originally emanated from developed countries but may have been re-engineered and adapted for use in new plants, as projects have to be individually designed and engineered to specific needs which vary according to location, raw materials, product range and labour skills. Such exports may involve India's expertise in pre project feasibility studies, basic process engineering and detailed designs for construction and training.

Argentina, Brazil, South Korea and Taiwan are involved in turnkey projects in steel, paper, petrochemicals, cement and food processing. While South Korean exporters of turnkey projects are large Chaebols, Argentinean exporters are medium sized companies.

Indian companies often try to exploit their technological ability while lagging behind in organisation. The South Korean companies export their superior organisation skills, though relatively deficient in technology. Taiwan's exports in this area evidence mastery over conventional production technology, intermediate capital intensity and small scale production. A more aggressive policy with greater feasibility in buying 'missing components' of technology from abroad may yield results in India's turnkey plant exports.

Outward Foreign Direct Investment

The export of technology may at times lead to foreign direct investment by developing countries often in neighbouring countries. Detailed data are often unavailable as many such investments are routed through tax havens like Panama, Bermuda, Bahamas, Hong Kong and Singapore. Indian FDI abroad is limited to indigenous technology and equipment mostly in the form of joint ventures with host country enterprises. Contribution from Indian companies are mostly in the form of plant and equipment for industries ranging from textiles, food, commercial vehicles, auto components, machinery and pharmaceuticals. India seems to lead third world countries in export of consultancy services. While such consultancies involve exports of Indian capital goods, more often, they tend towards procurement of foreign equipment.

Indian civil construction exports (non-industrial technology) depends more on organisation and management expertise than on technology. Most of such contracts have been in Middle East and Libya. Indian firms' experience in putting up large scale products however, is not supported by marketing acumen and financial support.

Garment Exports

India's garment exports seem to be healthy and growing in strength (US$ 2834 Million in 1994-95) but pale into insignificance in comparison to exports from Sri Lanka, and Bangladesh. The share of non-quota garments to quota countries is increasing though exporters are keen on quota categories as they bring in higher unit prices. To encourage non-quota exports, quota entitlement is offered as an incentive to exporters who fulfil non-quota targets.

The major constraints facing garment exports seems

to include lack of cohesive export policy, frequent policy changes (in quota entitlements), low value addition, unreliable deliveries and short term profit strategies.

Garments for exports are mostly made by the small scale sector, resulting in export of lower end cotton garments. Growth, however, implies new technology, higher value addition, economies of scale and higher inputs of labour and power.

The Indian exporter takes credit for little value addition. Forty percent of value is added at the designing stage by the foreign buyer. Fifty percent of value addition is by financiers and marketers and the remaining ten percent by the exporter who has little knowledge of the ultimate buyers and the market trend. The solution according to Mr. Koshi, Chairman, Apparel Marketing and Merchandising, National Institute of Fashion Technology is for exporters to integrate backwards into fabric manufacture.

Recent liberalisation offers wide scope for the industry to modernise, to seek foreign collaboration and joint ventures to improve its share of ready-mades in the world market above the current 2%. To improve its export performance in garments, the target market has to move up from the current low end towards the higher end of the market which would include synthetics and woollens in addition to cotton as also catering to autumn and winter wears. India should also aim at segments that are being vacated by countries like Taiwan and South Korea.

A recent survey holds out prospects for India, China, and Brazil with strong natural fibre base, acceptable technology level and skilled labour to play a leading role in world garment trade. With the discontinuation of the MFA by the year 2005, Indian garment exporters have to gear up to face a highly competitive quota-less world.

Electronic and Software Exports

The Indian software exports are a low cost option to in-house development in several developed countries. Though Indian software professionals can conceptualise and communicate well in English, their project management skills are weak and exposure to the latest technology is limited.

Indian exporters hardly have any packaged software that could gain international acceptance. But the small and medium size of the Indian companies provides them with strength to provide services, not products according to S. Srivastava, Chairman, Electronics and Computer Software Export Promotion Council (ESC).

Software Technology Parks (STPs—which are 100% export oriented) are located in Pune, Banglore, Bhubaneshwar, Hyderabad, Noida, Gandhinagar and Thiruvanantapuram. The STP provides infrastructure assistance to a number of units, offering facilities such as power, centralised computer environment and data collection facilities.

STPs are subject to export obligations but have the convenience of single window approvals, permission for 100% foreign equity, duty free imports, no value addition norms, permission for domestic tariff area (DTA) up to 25% of export value and exemption from corporate tax for five years out of eight years of the firms existence.

The electronic and computer software export promotion council estimates the sector's steady growth at 30% (US$ 116 million in 1994-95). The major markets consist of Germany, USA, UK, Spain, Dubai, South Africa and Australia. Exports are expected to touch Rs. 5000 crores in 1995-96.

Gems and Jewellery Exports

The success story of India's gems and jewellery exports

is a rare combination of the solid base created by our exporters as a result of the available skills of Indian artisans. It has brought enormous benefits to India in terms of employment, social uplift and rural development in small backward communities.

Export of gems and jewellery totalled US$ 5,276 million in the year 1995-96, an increase of 16.6% over 1994-95. The major markets are USA, Hong Kong, Belgium and Thailand while diamonds contributes to major share of gem and jewellery exports.

The diamond industry plans to shift focus from producing cut and polished diamonds to manufacturing and export of jewels. Diversification and increase in production base of gems and jewellery would enhance exports. It is also suggested that domestic tariff area (DTA) be brought on par with free trade zones.

Tourism

India has innumerable tourist attractions but tourist arrivals are kept small by inadequate hotel accommodation, poorly developed tourist infrastructure and insufficient marketing abroad. India's tourist earnings has been less than 0.5% of global tourist receipts and arrivals less than 2 million against Hong Kong's 8.9 million tourist arrivals.

The national tourism plan drawn up by New Delhi seeks to increase the number of foreign tourists to 5 million by the turn of the century which would require an increase in starred hotel rooms to 125,000.

The opening up of the economy has benefited the tourist industry, as massive influx of foreign business travellers has done away with the cyclical nature of the industry and the industry's foreign exchange earnings has recorded phenomenal growth of over 65%, with tourist arivals touching an all time high of 2.4 million. "The industry today, holds second position as the country's net foreign exchange earner" (Menna Nichani, The Economic Times, July 16, 1996).

From the preceding discussions it is apparent that a large number of agencies and institutions are engaged in the task of export promotion. Often the exporter finds himself lost in the midst of a jungle of such agencies and institutions, due to lack of co-ordination among them. The need for effective co-ordination in their policies and programmes cannot be over emphasised.

7.3 OVERVIEW OF SELECTED EXPORT MARKETS

Among the established markets for Indian exports identified as strategically more important than others are USA, the CIS, the UK, Hong Kong, Singapore and emerging markets like Myanmar. Some are not currently markets for high percentages of India's exports, but could help as catalysts for future expansion of Indian exports in certain markets geographically, politically or culturally linked to them.

7.3.1 USA

The USA is India's largest trading partner (20% of India's exports and 12% of imports) and Indo-US trade has been growing steadily since the reforms. The USA is a market for exports such as gems and jewellery, ready-made garments, cotton yarn, metal manufactures, cashew, carpets, handicrafts, drugs and pharmaceuticals, dyes and intermediaries and engineering goods.

Liberalisation has helped India become attractive for American investment and exports such as aircraft and components, fertilisers, organic chemicals, metaliferrous ores, telecommunications and petroleum exploration and refining equipment. The potential market of 920 million people is also an attraction for US manufacturers ranging from autos to fast food.

India has to cultivate this market and attune its export strategy to the consumer's and industries of the United States, both from the export point of view as well as attracting FDI, technology and international links.

The major concerns of Indian exporters are the large number of regulations—taxes, policies and legal instruments like section 301 of trade act of 1988. New US concerns in the areas of human rights, nuclear non-proliferation, social dumping and intellectual property protection are reflected in US imports.

India's export of invisible (46% of India's total export to US) has recorded an annual average rate of growth of 31%. The major items of invisibles in India's exports to US consist of travel, miscellaneous including technology and management, private transfers and transportation.

US has been demanding that India liberalise its financial markets (banking and insurance) while India fears that her banking and insurance industry could not survive competition from US financial and insurance industries. India on her part is asking for temporary movement of professionals and skilled labour. The US fears that this may create problems in immigration and this would call for change in law. A Californian court had dismissed a case against Tata Consultancy Services, charging them with depressing American wages by bringing Indian software engineers to work in the United States. The court further pointed out that Indian engineers indirectly would help establish US products and introduce US companies into India.

7.3.2 Commonwealth of Independent States (CIS)

Economic liberalisation, both in CIS and India portends growth for trade between the two friendly countries.

Indian exports to erstwhile USSR were little over Rs. 210 crores in 1970-71, rising to Rs. 2004 crores in 1993-94. However, since the break-up of the USSR, Indo-Russian trade suffered low and irregular growth. The trade seems to be subject to many complexities and contradictions such as multiplicity of trade channels operating simultaneously. Trade is accounted under debt repayment rupee account, escrow account, hard currency account and the semi-legal or underground channel. Many of the Indian exports enter Russia through more than one channel, making it extremely difficult to estimate exactly.

The major problems faced by Indian exporters are many. Multiplicity of channels, lack of transparency on release of debt payment rupee funds, uncertainties in Russia's tax structure and import regulations, underdeveloped banking structure and lack of specialised Indian agencies to export specialised products.

The potential for Indo-Russian trade is immense, though many Indian firms have withdrawn from Moscow after the disintegration of the USSR. Both the governments of India and CIS could deliberate on development of economic relations, in view of their past close relationships in may areas including defence. Indian companies should also set long term objectives and aim at joint ventures in many areas including banking to benefit from the Russian market.

The five Central Asian republics Kazakhstan, Tajikastan, Turkmesnistan, Uzbekistan and Kirghizistan currently in transition are likely to settle down as prospective markets as they are strong in mineral resources and agriculture products. These countries are rebuilding their economies and offer immense possibilities of co-operation in economic, technological and cultural fields.

7.3.3 Singapore

Singapore is a natural bridge-head to further Indian business interests in the booming economies of the Pacific Rim and *vice versa*. The canvas of mutual business interests is a wide one covering bilateral trade, shipping, ports and infrastructure development, financial services, real estate and property development among many others.

Singapore, with its Indian Diaspora, and successful Indian business, has a close cultural link with India and close geographical proximity to east coast and Tamil Nadu which could help.

7.3.4 Hong Kong

The Hong Kong Trade Development Council (TDC), supported by the Hong Kong government had evinced interest in establishing links with India's trading community. Several delegations visited India (1995-96) and have already established business. TDC has plans to set up two offices in Bombay and Delhi to foster further links between Hong Kong and India. The Indian trading community in Hong Kong (which controls a good percentage of Hong Kong's exports that peaked at 12%) is an important factor.

Hong Kong has much to offer in the form of expertise and investment infrastructure upgrading "priorities also include export manufacturing" according to Victor Lo in which Hong Kong's successful experience in China would be of benefit to India. The Indian market has a number of similarities to China in terms of its size, a large pool of available labour and abundant natural resources.

Stage of development need high technology. Hong Kong's experience in export manufacturing serves it well to harness these elements. "The same formula of Hong Kong capital, technology, managerial and marketing know-how" can combine with India's land and labour in joint partnership. Hong Kong companies have the backing of a major financial centre (with 85 of world's 100 major banks) to raise investment funds for off-shore projects. Hong Kong companies have proven themselves among the most flexible and adaptable in the world, despite bureaucracy, infrastructure shortcomings and government restrictions in countries such as India.

On the positive side, Indian business can use Hong Kong as a conduit for doing business with China, Taiwan and other countries in East Asia.

Jardines Matheson, one of the biggest Hongs (conglomerates) have invested 20% in Tata services for infrastructure development in India. Many medium and small business already have an investment base in India. For outward oriented Indian business, Hong Kong could be a diving board into the vastly growing Asian markets and the association will be mutually rewarding.

With over 22,000 Indians in Hong Kong, with British or Indian passports, have been looking for alternative investments after the hand over of Hong Kong to mainland China in July 1997, though there is no panic emigration. Many Indian business houses in Hong Kong have business interests in Dubai, Singapore or Bangkok and some have established manufacturing operations in India. However, Hong Kong business used to governments' "positive non-intervention" policy in Hong Kong, find the going tough in India, and as a result, Hong Kong Indian investment has been mostly in property and the stock market.

The major constraints and barriers faced by them seem to be in the red tape, bureaucratic hurdles, commitment to schedules and undertakings. According to a leading businessman Mr. Hatim Ebrahim, "it is not a one window situation, it is not even one house." Another complaint has been the failure of the Indian government to match their enthusiasm in investing in India and ministers and officials passing through Hong Kong do not even address Indian businessmen on the opportunities that India offers. The diplomatic mission in Hong Kong is not able to furnish information and India does not have a trade office in Hong Kong.

7.3.5 United Kingdom

As early as 1907, Tatas set up an office in London and London today serves as a gateway to the growing EU market. Many Indian enterprises have recently followed suit as they discover that London is a major window to the world. Companies such as Reliance, SIEL Overseas, Kotak Mahindra, Garware, DCM Shriram and Essar have set up offices in London for liasing with customers in EU and Africa. EU is the most important market for Indian exports, especially as EU is likely to expand its membership in the future.

7.3.6 New Frontiers

Several markets have developed as new frontiers for India's exports since the 1990s. These markets may currently be of limited significance but are likely to come into prominence due to geo-political and social factors.

7.3.6.1 Myanmar

Myanmar, cut off from the world for over quarter of a century has of late been discovered by several Indian industrial houses, planning investment in tyres, paper, pulp, textiles etc.

Myanmar could become a strategic base for taking on contiguous markets like China to the north, ASEAN across the border. Garware's plans to utilise bamboo into making much needed pulp which will be exported to India. The country's abundance of natural resources, ranging from heavy teak and hard wood forests to oil and gas deposits, could attract Indian investment and trade. The attractions include a large market of 45 million (though GDP/ capita is a low $220), a surprisingly high literacy rate of 80% and a familiarity with the English language and legal system. Myanmar has been referred to by National Geographic as "the richest of poor countries" and a 'bejewelled pauper', needs virtually everything : consumer goods, intermediate and capital goods. 'The sky is the limit for Indian companies' a Senior commerce ministry official observed.

The "deep suspicion of Indian quality and lingering distrust of Indians from the colonial days" is yielding place to business connection due to increased high level exchanges. Border trading posts at Moreh and Champhal help speeding dispatches into western Myanmar, and accounts for $100 - $150 m. Air links from Calcutta and Madras is likely to establish trade relations. India has agreed to build a road from Moreh to Kaleymo, 60 km from Mandalay. This would help entry into a new market for Indian goods. With a booming construction industry, India could emerge as a supplier of cement and steel. One half of Myanmar, east of Irrawaddy river is influenced by Chinese goods.

7.3.6.2 Morocco

This North African nation offers an opening into the Maghreb countries (Algeria, Tunisia, Libya, Mauritania) as well as access to the European markets. Imports into Morocco is virtually license free and attracts very low tariff. The Moroccan government is stable, with an economy that is increasingly being liberalised and import oriented. The free zone at Tangiers, 13 km from Spain, offers incentives for setting up export bases and has a good infrastructure and efficient port facilities.

7.3.6.3 Tunisia

Tunisia also offers opportunities for processing and re-export due to geographical proximity to Europe as well 'Tunisia's special trade arrangements with African countries like Senegal, Mali, Chad, Niger as well as close trading links with Jordan, Syria and Egypt. Tunisia's global imports are over US$ 5 billion.

7.3.6.4 South Africa

It is most industrial and economically advanced country in Africa, a potential active collaborator with Indian industry and joint venture partner in thirty four sub-Saharan countries. South Africa's imports which total US$ 20 billion and 15 lakh people of Indian origin, offer an attractive market. It is estimated that South Africa can provide a market of US$ 4-5 billion by the year 2000 AD for Indian products.

7.4 EXPORT PROMOTION—CO-ORDINATION THE KEY

Industries which have vast export potential have been suffering acute and widespread sickness such as Textiles, Engineering, jute and chemicals. More earnest attempts at alleviating such selected industries are called for.

Omkar Goswami Committee said that "Not only are large and medium scale units getting sick, but they are also locking up increasing amounts of nominal and real bank credit. N.A. Palkiwala once referred to the 'absolute instability and uncertainty of our tax system' every year. Sometimes even within half a year, some changes are made in the income tax act.

The Chelliah Committee suggested that changes in the laws should be kept to a minimum once in 5 years—after public debate except for special cases calling for immediate change. Practice of changes in each years' budget should be given up.

7.5 WHAT AILS OUR EXPORTS?

Foreign exchange conservation is indeed a crucial topic discussed and ideas on policies, plans, strategies and procedures have been forthcoming from statesmen, politicians, bureaucrats, businessmen and consultants on ways and means of integration of the Indian economy with global business. Export is a war where the details are to be taken care of and matters which may seem trifle often turn to be crucial. We have a good climate of policies, plans and strategies spoiled by procedural bottlenecks which deters many of our small and medium size exporters. We have about 2 lakh exporters but 95% of our exports are through 4000 exporters.

Fixation of input/output norms take months resulting in delay in issuance of advanced licence and execution of exports. Licensing authorities insist on either a bond or letter of undertaking and any minor change later on causes delay. Redemption of the bond after export takes months blocking bank accounts.

Export/Import policy and procedures are advised through different notifications (about 12) and are difficult to keep track of, especially by small and medium size exporters. Bureaucratic attitude seems negative and insist on attention to minute details.

Currently, all export contracts are to be registered with Export Promotion Councils and non-registration may result in customs with holding shipments. Colleciton of statistical data could be made simpler.

No central agency is available to clarify details of procedure. Exporter has to seek information from RBI, Licensing Authority, Customs, Central Excise, Export Promotion Council. Hence, a central information desk is called for to avoid inordinate delay in disposal of deemed exports benefit claims. Simplifications of regulation on indirect taxes (Central Excise, Salt and Customs Act) are needed urgently.

7.6 EXPORTS—THE KEY TO INDIA'S GROWTH

Benevolent role that exports played in India's long term development has not been fully recognised. Earlier, luke warm support to exports along with concentration on import substitution affected availability of even some essential items. This resulted in production being concentrated in the hands of a few industrial houses and technology was not upgraded. Lack of a well thought out export program lost many opportunities in international trade by sticking to import substitution and domestic self sufficiency.

Similarly, large investments in public sector failed to make any significant mark on industrial growth though the potential of the private sector could have been tapped more vigorously. The continued BOP problem led to a crisis situation in 1990 calling for a bold export policy with increased assistance to the domestic manufacturers to compete effectively in the international markets. The export expansion program should be self sustaining based on competition, cost structure as well as production of quality products.

India's development strategy in industrial and agricultural policies has been structured to achieve the objective of acceleration of Indian exports. Unless the growing presure on imports (petroleum and fertilisers being major items) is reduced, the BOP position will continue to cost concern.

7.7. CONCLUSION

In this chapter, an attempt has been made to suggest how some of the export promotion policies, schemes, incentives and measures could be adapted so that they could yield the expected and desired results for Indian exporters as well as the nation.

However, in view of the drastically changed and dynamically changing international situation, it is well nigh clear that India has to evolve a totally new approach and new model of export promotion strategies for the future. That forms the subject matter of the following chapter.

CHAPTER 8

FUTURE MODEL OF EXPORT PROMOTION STRATEGIES IN INDIA

8.1 INTRODUCTION

In recent years much thought has been given at the highest level in India to evolve a totally new approach—a new strategy for promoting India's exports not only quantitatively but also qualitatively, consistent with the dimensions of export profitability, for a continuous improvement in gross and net terms of trade and international relations favourable to India. Four different strategies have been suggested by the Board of Trade (1991), ASSOCHAM (1993), FICCI (1995) and the Commerce Ministry of the Government of India (1995). In the following paragraphs, the new strategies for export promotion has been brought under sharp focus for careful and critical evaluation.

There has been consensus among government, business and academicians that to bring in faster growth of exports, India has to launch a strategy focusing on selected products and countries rather than spread export effort across the whole range of commodities. An extreme focus concept was developed by several organisations though the point of focus varies from one another.

Estimates of sustainable export growth ranged from 10% - 25% annual growth rate and the target export value to be reached by the year 2000 ranged from US$ 86 - 100 billion. The Ministry of Commerce seems to be optimistic of reaching a share of 1% of world exports which would be around US$ 90 billion by 2002, as indicated in the medium term export strategies (97-98).

8.2 EXTREME FOCUS STRATEGY—BOARD OF TRADE

The Board of Trade in December 1991 deliberated a strategy which identified 34 products as having the potential for faster growth. As many as 26 working groups constituted for the purpose studied these sectors in detail and put forth some 500 recommendations, which were scrutinised and put up as agenda for implementation. The strategy covered policy issues, procedural simplifications, infrastructure improvements and institutional arrangements. Pursuant to the recommendations, several measures have been taken by the Government comprising trade policy and fiscal, credit, infrastructural, institutional and administrative arrangements. Specific mention may be made of unified market determined exchange rate system, reduction in import duty on specified capital goods from 40% to 25%, reduction in import duty on raw materials, increase in availability of export credit at lower rates of interest, opening of inland container depots and container freight stations. Institutional arrangements like setting up six task forces which covered agriculture and agro products, electronics and information technology, textiles, garments and chemicals, pharmaceuticals and granite need to be mentioned. Administrative measures comprising setting up of exporters' grievances redress cells were also recommended.

Thirty four extreme focus products and product groups identified were expected to record an increase of 30% in value or volume each year. The product categories identified were :

1. Indian products where India enjoyed a share of

more than 1% of world exports, and could be a big player.

2. Familiar 'stars' —Products in which though India was a small player, had the wherewithal for future growth.
3. 'Sunrise Products' —Products in which India lacks knowledge and experience, but which offer enormous opportunities for growth.

The products identified were agriculture, agro-chemicals, auto components, bicycles and cement, complete vehicles, drugs and pharmaceuticals, dyes and intermediates, electric power generation and distribution equipment, floriculture, footwear, fresh fruits, gold jewellery, granite, hand tools, IC engines and parts, industrial castings and forgings, tomato paste products, tropical fruit juices, pulp and concentrates, preserved mushrooms (processed foods), ready made garments, Rice, software packages, system software, network, CAD/CAM software, spices, sugar, molasses, alcohol including ethyl alcohol, sugar machinery, synthetic and man made textiles and tyres- in all 34 product groups and items.

Appropriate institutional mechanism was to be developed followed by highly visible endeavours by industry and trade with the government providing a liberalised, market friendly environment. Export surpluses were to be generated through quality upgradation and increased productivity.

One of the many criticisms of the Extreme Focus Strategy was that the number of items (34) was found to be very large. Certain products do not deserve to be in focus and a few others to be considered as sub sectors. Some products contribute to a minuscule annual exports (tomato paste US$50,000 or tropical fruits (US$ 2 million) and should not have been in the list. Other products like sugar are highly susceptible to vagaries of monsoon (export ranged from US$ 50 to US$ 111 million), while some items like molasses and alcohol showed poor exports.

The extreme focus items which registered a consistent growth for at least three years (though nowhere near the minimum 30%) included fisheries, automotive components, dyes and intermediates, garments, synthetic and man made textiles, tyres, rice, cement and granite.

8.3 ASSOCHAM SUGGESTIONS

In a seminar on "Doubling exports in select focus product groups by 96-97", on 14th August 1993 organised by the Associated Chambers of Commerce and Industry of India, the foreign trade committee of ASSOCHAM suggested concentration on five out of thirty four extreme focus areas already identified by the board of trade. These sectors included :

1. Agricultural/Agro- processing industry and allied sector
2. Leather and leather products
3. Electronics and Information Technology
4. Textiles and Garments
5. Chemicals, pharmaceuticals and granite

The above was based on ASSOCHAM's reading of encouraging portents that India's exports were well on their way to scaling new heights by early 1993-94 (against poor export growth of 3.6% in 1992-93). ASSOCHAM felt it crucial that for acquiring visibility on the external front, exports should grow in dollar terms by at least 22% annually till 2000A.D. to normalise imbalance in Balance of Payment (BOP).

ASSOCHAM was of the view that a big push in India's exports is not beyond our capacity and doubling of exports by 96-97 was possible since the level of exports in 1993 was only about 0.41% of the world exports. However another strategy was formulated after about two years.

8.4 STRATEGY FOR SATURATION MARKETING

On the 27th of December 1995, the commerce minister, Shri. P. Chidambaram unveiled a new short term export promotion strategy on 27th December, 1995 which focused attention on 15 product and 15 country matrix with the aim to step up export earnings between US$ 75 and 80 billion by 2000 AD. The commerce minister's presentation focused on the idea of diversifying the export markets and products and to concentrate on the principal markets so that the products could be well established. The exercise identifies 225 markets and products though in effect, there are only 200 as the value of exports for certain products are negligible.

The commerce ministry has found that in 94-95, out of a total exports of US$26.2 billion, US$ 19.29 billion went to these 15 markets out of which US$ 13.12 billion was accounted for by the 15 products. The new strategy focuses mainly on consumer products rather than spread the resources thinly over a wide range of products and markets.

The 15 products comprised of gems and jewellery, RMC cotton and accessories, cotton yarn fabrics and made ups, marine products, drugs and pharmaceuticals, transport equipment, metal manufactures, machinery and instruments, leather manufactures, man-made yarn, fabrics and made ups, oil meals, leather footwear, dyes and intermediaries, as well as plastic and linoleum products.

The top 15 destinations included USA, Japan, Germany, UK, Hong Kong, UAE, Belgium, Italy, Russia,

Singapore, Bangladesh, Netherlands, France, Saudi-Arabia and Thailand.

It was found that 72% of India's exports to USA were concentrated in eleven products. The percentage for Japan, Germany, the UK, Hong Kong, the UAE, Belgium, Italy, Russia, Singapore, Bangladesh, the Netherlands, France, Saudi Arabia and Thailand ranges between 62% and 92% for 11 products. A similar exercise for the 15 thrust products showed that exports of gems and jewellery are concentrated to the extent of 94.4% in all the countries. The range for the other 14 products varied from 53% to 90%. Among the winning products especially important to India, gem and jewellery ranked as the top product in five markets, number two in two markets and lower in three markets. Ready made cotton garments were first in four markets, second in two markets and lower in five.

The USA is the top destination for Indian products, topping in seven of the fifteen thrust products. The USA is also a significant market for fourteen of the fifteen products barring oil meals. After the USA, Japan is rated as the second major market where tariffs range from 5-10%. Germany, the UK, Belgium, Italy, the Netherlands and France are the major markets in the European Union. Germany is the third major market in most of the products followed by the UK (No.4), Belgium (No.7), Italy (No.8), the Netherlands (No.12) and France (No.13). Hong Kong ranks as the fifth largest destination for Indian products and being a free port, most of Indian exports do not attract tariffs. The UAE being the sixth major market for Indian products, is emerging as an important trading centre for Hong Kong exports. The tariff rate ranges from 0-4%. Russia used to be a very good destination for Indian exports, but after the disintegration of USSR, exports have been fluctuating. Singapore's importance as a trading partner with India lies in its location as well as membership of ASEAN. Singapore allows duty-free entry for most of Indian products. Saudi Arabia is considered as the fourteenth largest market in the matrix and tariffs range from 0-20%. Thailand figures as the fifteenth largest market in the matrix of exports.

The commerce minister stated that these products and markets will be pushed aggressively by about 200 export facilitators financed by the India Brand Equity Fund. These facilitators would be designated for each focus product in each country and will be responsible for helping boost exports. Their responsibilities include market surveys to gauge consumer preferences, along with identifying and tackling tariff and non-tariff barriers. The facilitator could be either a bilateral chamber of commerce or an export promotion council or even an individual or a company dealing with that product. In case an individual or a company is appointed, more than 1 facilitator may be designated. A provision of Rs. 70 crore towards promotion of the matrix products in the matrix markets was provided for.

Regarding the conclusions from the study of the matrix, the commerce ministry further suggested that :

1. There is no shame in exporting consumer products and each country should export what it can.
2. India should concentrate on markets with a per capita income of US$ 20,000.
3. Effort should be made to increase the country's share in markets where it already has a presence.
4. If one product finds an entry into a market, it should be possible to enlarge the range of products.
5. If one product is established in a particular country, it might be possible to introduce the product in neighbouring countries as well.

8.5 SUGGESTIONS FROM THE FEDERATION OF INDIAN CHAMBERS OF COMMERCE AND INDUSTRY

At a symposium on "Export vision : 2001" organised by FICCI on 26th July, 1995 at Delhi, an export target of US$ 96 billion by the year 2001 was considered attainable. The product groups selected for focused promotion were nine in number with growth targets ranging from 25% to a maximum of 35% which are as follows :

1. Agri Products
2. Textiles & garments
3. Engineering goods such as auto components, hand tools, certain machine tools, two-wheelers, consumer durables, etc.
4. Electronics and computer software
5. Chemicals and pharmaceuticals
6. Granite and construction materials
7. Leather manufactures
8. Gems & jewellery
9. Handicrafts

The markets selected for particular attention were ten in number out of 24 markets identified as prospective included USA, Japan, Germany, UK., Hong Kong, UAE, Belgium, Italy, Russia (CIS), and Singapore.

In addition to India's traditional markets of Europe, America, Japan, West Asia and ASEAN, following emerging markets were also recommended for exploring potential. South Africa, Israel, Russia and CIS countries, China, Taiwan and Iran.

Having looked at the several strategies proposed by the Board of Trade, ASSOCHAM, FICCI, and the Ministry of Commerce, Government of India, there seems to be divergence in approach. The Government's strategy was found to contain certain flaws. Focusing on 15 countries would dilute the impact of focus, hence a reduced number nearer 10 would be more appropriate. The number could be increased to next 10 countries in the second phase, and another 5 in the third phase. Again a list of 15 products proposed for concentrated attention appears large to begin with. This could be reduced to 10 in the first phase, another 10 in the second phase and 5 in the third phase. The fifteen products included within the Commerce Ministry's matrix belong to product groups in which India has been traditionally strong. In view of the liberalisation the product range should necessarily include non traditional items (where value addition must be higher and terms of trade better). Export Promotion Strategy is not to be decided on economic profit-loss basis, but has to be viewed as an element of total national policy of international relations. Foreign Trade is often influenced by factors like geography, politics, history and social relations in addition to economics. The selection of countries may have to be made against this background, on the basis of India's present position and future requirements. During the year 1997-98, the Ministry of Commerce has come out with an improved strategy called "Medium Term Export Strategy, against the background of recent slowdown in world export growth in general and slowdown in India's exports witnessed since June 1996. This strategy has been highlighted earlier in Chapter 5.

8.6 PROJECTION OF EXPORT PERFORMANCE

Individual business organisations, government departments and planning commission have projected different attainable export targets by the turn of the century. Based on 1980-82 export figures, performance of export at 5% is unacceptable when world trade is expected to grow at the rate of 9.8%. To carve a 1% share of world exports by 2000 AD, India may have to reach US$ 96 billion at an average annual growth of 25%. Sceptics consider this rate not maintainable, though in terms of potential, it is not beyond reach. This would entail sustained efforts from both government and business.

Others opine that world trade would grow faster due to freer trade under WTO regime. The growth in exports is accompanied by a higher rate of growth in imports, which has to be lowered and maintained at 20% if a balance of trade is to be achieved by the year 2000-2001.

Growth rates in exports for the period 1989 to 1997 as estimated by K. Krishnamoorthy *et al.*, of Delhi School of Economics (E & PW, March 16, 1996) are :

Year	*Export Growth (%)*
1989 (89-90)	18.92
1990	8.98
1991	-1.14
1992	3.30
1993	20.30
1994	17.89
1995	21.12
1996	21.01
1997	22.58

On this basis, it may not be possible to sustain a rate of growth at 25% but a 22% growth seems more likely. But recent growth rates (4% in 1997-98, with US$34B) in exports have belied these optimistic expectations. And projection of 20% growth in 1997-98 by the Commerce Ministry early in the years is considered unattainable.

8.7 CONCLUSION

This chapter related the different estimates of export performance based on a largely consensual approach of focusing export promotion on limited number of products and countries, so as to gain a faster rate of growth in the immediate future. The trend during the past years would justify such a move. More difficult would be to maintain the sustained growth, which will depend on many factors, internal and external. The concluding part in the next chapter would outline further recommendations towards achieving the projected optimistic targets.

Table 8.1

Present Top Ten Markets For Indian Exports

Country	*Exports in 1997-98 (US$ Million)*
USA	6638
UK	2041
Hong Kong	1922
Germany	1857
Japan	1860
UAE	1597
Belgium	1192
Singapore	740
Italy	1100
Russia	890

Source : Centre for Monitoring Indian Economy, Bombay.

Table 8.2

India's Share in Selected Countries, 1996

Value : $ Billion

Country	*Total Import (1996)*	*Import from India (1996-97)*	*India's Share (%)*
EUROPE			
Germany	456.3	1.86	0.41
UK	287.5	2.03	0.71
France	275.6	0.71	0.26
Italy	207	0.92	0.44
Neitherland	180.7	0.84	0.46
ASIA & OCEANIA			
Japan	349.2	1.99	0.57
HongKong	201.3	0.86	0.92
Singapore	131.3	0.96	0.73
South Korea	150.2	0.5	0.33
Thailand	73.5	0.44	0.6
Malaysia	78.6	0.52	0.66
Indonesia	42.9	0.58	1.35
AMERICA			
USA	817.8	6.54	0.80
Canada	175.2	0.35	0.2
EMERGING MARKETS			
China	138.8	0.59	0.42
Israel	31.3	0.21	0.67
South Africa	30.1	0.32	1.06
UAE	24.6	1.47	5.97
Iran	14.5	0.19	1.31

Source : WTO : *Annual Report* 1996 & Table 2.15.

Table 8.3

India's Product-Wise Growth

Product	*Percent Growth in 1996-97 over previous year*
Agri Products	6.23
Textiles and Garments	6.99
Engineering Products	9.26
Electronics & Computer Software	13.11
Chemicals & Related Products	7.40
Gems and Jewellery	10.06
Leather and Manufactures	11.31
Handicrafts	8.96

Source : Ministry of Commerce, Government of India & DGCI&S.

Table 8.4

Principal Exports Registering Positive and Negative Growth

(Rs. Crore)

Rank based on 1997-98 data	*Commodity*	*1996-97*	*1997-98*	*Percentage change in 1997-98 over 1996-97*
1	Gems & jewellery	16,872	19,014	12.70
2	Cotton yarn, fabrics, made-ups etc.	11,082	12,094	9.13
3	RMG cotton including accessories	10,439	10,429	(-)neg
4	Drugs, pharmaceuticals & fine chemicals	4,342	5,228	20.41
5	Machinery and instruments	3,753	4,314	14.95
6	Marine products	4,008	4,313	7.61
7	Manufactures of metals	3,243	3,985	22.88
8	Oilmeals	3,495	3,404	(-)2.60
9	Transport equipments	3,439	3,117	(-)9.36
10	Manmade yarn, fabrics and made-ups	2,494	2,854	14.43
11	Electronic goods	2,782	2,400	(-)13.73
12	Primary & semi-finished iron & steel	2,183	2,394	9.67
13	RMG manmade fibres	1,801	2,313	28.43
14	Dyes, intermediates and coal tar chemicals	1,995	2,228	11.68
15	Inorganic and agro-chemicals	1,971	2,195	11.36
16	Handicrafts (excluding handmade carpets)	1,986	1,927	14.09
17	Plastic & Iinoleum products	1,915	1,904	(-)0.57
18	Iron ore	1,706	1,763	3.34
19	Basmati rice	1,248	1,674	34.13
20	Coffee	1,427	1,622	13.67

Source : DGCI & S Calcutta.

Table 8.5

India's Exports to 15 Emerging Markets

(Rs. Crore)

	Country	*1992-93*	*1993-94*	*1994-95*	*1995-96*	*1996-97*	*1997-98*
1.	Singapore	1,704.55	2,358.64	2,418.61	3,015.94	3,470.01	2,746.12
2.	Canada	553.56	714.64	837.88	1,021.67	1,253.11	1,548.88
3.	Malaysia	549.80	775.67	899.53	1,315.11	1,885.52	1,788.51
4.	Chinese Taipei	517.03	865.14	787.47	861.44	1,504.11	1,443.74
5.	Switzerland	576.56	693.13	776.77	941.78	1,064.56	1,389.12
6.	Australia	646.45	769.25	1,0877.79	1,256.56	1,368.00	1,581.69
7.	China, P. Rep.	409.18	875.32	798.24	1,112.88	2,182.54	2,530.88
8.	South Afirca	4.70	80.73	491.47	1,102.23	1,122.48	1,426.80
9.	Israel	246.47	413.61	471.79	724.39	750.50	1,222.58
10.	Thailand	734.59	1,118.12	1,276.64	1,581.91	1,587.12	1,254.66
11.	Turkey	300.64	351.99	299.10	575.22	716.52	870.06
12.	Korea, Rep.	506.47	647.47	1,043.82	1,499.41	1,840.58	1,530.00
13.	Egypt, A. Rep.	330.84	379.58	376.18	549.42	558.96	947.45
14.	Nigeria	418.87	374.09	342.65	504.73	519.88	794.22
15.	Mexico	124.93	178.20	245.74	183.37	277.91	404.53

Source : DGCI & S (various issues), Calcutta.

Chapter 9

Findings, Conclusions and Recommendations

9.1 INTRODUCTION

At the time of Independence of India, 'a developing country' was considered synonymous with 'raw material exporter', and early planners held that industrialisation was to be aimed at the domestic market. India was one of the early developing countries to industrialise and despite accelerating growth and development, her share of global exports has declined. The real reason is that her export growth was slower compared to other developing countries especially when compared to the growth of East Asian economies.

During the last two decades, the developing countries' share in manufactured exports rose sharply, mostly to developed markets. Indian manufactured exports have grown faster than OECD countries since 1980, but other developing countries continue to outpace her. In 1965, Indonesia and Thailand barely exported any manufactures—by 1985, their combined manufactured exports exceeded India's. By the year 1990, Thailand's alone exceeded that of India's and by 1992, each of them exported more manufactures than India, the combined value of their exports being three times that of India. It may be appropriate at this point to analyse the possible causes for this relative lapse on India's export efforts.

'Self-sufficiency' was an avowed aim of India's economic policies and seems to rear its head on and off. Excessive protectionism has been blamed but protectionism was practised in various degrees by several East Asian economies, combined with pressure on manufacturers to export. With protectionism, fewer imports would come in, reducing the level of exports needed for reaching balance of payment equilibrium. The effect could be high exchange rates (high domestic prices in foreign exchange terms) and export sales bringing in lower profits. Mr. Martin Woolf (Financial Times, London) explained the problem succinctly. Given protectionism, incentives received by would be exporters were less than what is offered by the domestic market. Devaluation raising the earnings from exports would reverse the relationship.

Today, Indian wage rates seem competitive to that of East Asian Countries like Hong Kong, Malaysia and Thailand, but their garment exports are advancing faster than India, despite the higher wages. Perhaps what counts is cost of labour determined by wage rate and productivity. Dearth of skills does not seem to be a problem in India, due to the large pool of educated people available at low, middle and high skill levels.

India's value addition to manufacturing sector has only exceeded one fourth in 1990 whereas, in Korea, it is 2/3, as in several European economies. The central issue is not absolute but relative, whether the export promotion policies are favourable enough to induce and enable exporters to produce at a rate comparable to other developing countries. Indian exporters today have to match the cost structure of their products to that of other developing countries like PRC as they are the real competitors in developed markets.

Comparison of a representative Indian firm *vis a vis* a

Korean firm, the difference in cost structure appears wide. Average cost of production as percentage of output value at world prices is 138 in India against 98 in South Korea. At a selling price of 100, the Indian firm has a cost disadvantage of 30% and even when export incentives are taken into account, the net profit is likely to be very low. This could only be corrected by improving productivity, reducing overheads, adjusting exchange rates and a reduction in input costs.

India's Competitiveness

The Geneva based World Economic Forum (WEF) in its Global Competitiveness Report 1996 (GCR) ranks India 45 among 49 countries, ahead of only Russia, Brazil, Venezuela and Hungary. The ranking was 35th in 1994, 39 in 1995 and 45th in 1996, a continuous decline. Singapore and Hong Kong are ranked first and second respectively. The study details India's ranking in over 155 parameters, 41 of them based on objective data and 114 of them on a survey of 2000 managers in the 49 countries. Broad range of factors were measured for estimating competitiveness such as openness, technology management, labour and civil institutions, each of which is assigned a different weight.

India's ranking in openness is 43 and India has to catch up with integrating into regional trade blocs, lifting quotas, improving access to international distribution mechanisms, permitting cross-border alliances and entering foreign capital markets.

India has improved its ranking in government factor to 20 from 30 in 1995 partly due to tax reforms. The negative factors are the inability to balance the budget and bureaucratic hindrance to business conduct.

On the finance parameter, India had slipped to 33rd rank in 1996 from 27 in 1994 due to the high cost of capital, high interest rates, risky financial markets and inefficient banking system.

India's infrastructure is ranked 48 out of 49 just behind Russia. Medium term infrastructure requirements are not reflected in government policies and mismatch between intent and execution in admitting private capital into infrastructure is in evidence.

Despite the large pool of scientists and engineers and rated as the sixth most preferred home for R&D, lack of financial incentives and absence of a research culture ranks India 35th on the technology factor.

Under the management factor, India has slipped from 39 in 1995 to 43 in 1996, due to weakness in total quality management, customer orientation, management practices and inadequate use of information technology. Her management asset is the innovative, entrepreneurial class. India's large man power and low wages earn a 33 rank. But the government's inability to introduce an exit policy and poor training facilities are seen as the negative factors.

The judicial and political institutions are adjudged as needing improvement on product liability and in adaptability of political system to economic changes, India is considered weak.

The ranking also reveals the prerequisites for high growth as a government that promotes but not participates in business, job creation and puts a premium on knowledge and information. (Business Today, June 22, 1996)

To sum up, one could hypothesise the causes of India's failure to keep up with export boom of developing countries :

- Manufacturing was essentially geared to

satisfying the needs of India's domestic market.

- Protectionistic policies reinforced the undemanding (especially in quality) nature of the market hence Indian products fell back against international standards of quality.
- Inward orientation had delayed and reduced the impetus to venture into export which is considered more risky.
- Foreign exchange and protection regime along with overall economic and political system stood in the way of accumulation and reinvestment of profits.
- Infrastructure like land transportation, telecommunications, harbour capacity affect domestic manufacturers as well as exporters and India is behind many newcomers.
- The productive efficiency of the domestic sector has indeed affected the productivity and competitiveness of Indian products in the international markets.

9.2 FINDINGS, RECOMMENDATIONS AND CONCLUSIONS

9.2.1 Findings

Chapter number five examined the gamut of export promotion schemes ranging from finance to transportation and subsidies. Compared to export promotion in other developing countries around the world, especially Asia, India seems to have tried almost all of promotional strategies. But the export figures do not appear to be commensurate with the extent of the incentives. This could be attributed to the poor implementation of the schemes rather than their inadequacies. The impact of export promotion strategy has to a large extent been blunted by the intricate bureaucracy and the complicated institutional framework.

A study of the economy and its uneven growth combined with deceleration of exports has largely been due to the inward looking policies followed by successive governments and the lack of emphasis on the export sector.

The reforms since 1991 has to a large extent attempted to confront the problems by bringing down barriers to import and emphasising the role of exports. The need of the hour is to implement the existing strategies vigorously, while searching for alternate and innovative measures in export promotion to make up for time lost towards regaining the position India held in International trade in the beginning of this century.

9.2.2 Recommendations

While modifications and improvements to many of the export promotion programs have been suggested earlier, the following recommendations would relate to future policies and their executive and administrative aspects.

Export orientation should permeate all aspects of India's trade philosophy, policies and executive and administrative branches. Such orientation should seep in from the top echelon to the shop floor as is evident in many countries like Taiwan, South Korea and Hong Kong. Often it is found that the enthusiasm in promoting exports is lost as we move down the administrative ladder. The 'Swadeshi' concept, while exhorting Indians to consume more national products, should not be allowed to stand in the way of developing production and marketing for export. It has also to be emphasised that the export sector cannot be developed in isolation while the rest of the economy lags behind. The problem facing the Indian economy especially in raising production to internationally acceptable standards is immense and may have to be tackled in stages—short, medium and long term.

9.2.2.1 Short Term

Consensus has to be developed in identifying the thrust sectors and markets to be focused upon, as several organisations and the commerce ministry recommend different targets. The first line of target sectors and markets to be followed by a second line so that India will have a continuous line of products and markets to focus upon, for development. Towards this intensive international research on prospective markets and products is called for so that strategies can be adapted to changing market environments.

9.2.2.2 Medium Term

Export policies are to be discussed with all concerned before finalisation and should be of sufficient duration so that exporters and manufacturers in turn can plan ahead their export operations. Closer consultations between government, business, exporters, academics, practising economists and foreign importers before major policy changes are needed. A more pragmatic rather than ideological approach is recommended. Such round table discussions to be publicised so that the general public would be aware of the export policies.

Percentage of value addition and incremental foreign exchange earnings to be made an important criteria in deciding on support to exports. Ultimate goal to be withdrawal of all subsidies, as India becomes competitive in the international market. Policy on subsidies to be monitored continuously for efficacy and subsidy fund to revolve between the current matrix and the following matrix.

Import contents of exports to be rationalised and

level of value addition to be related to export assistance.

Improved EPZ operation offering special facilities for joint ventures and foreign investors to be planned. Model industries to be set up in EPZ by attracting multinationals as in technology parks or Mexican Maquiladoras with a view to encourage re-exports.

9.2.2.3 Long Term

Export culture to be built up over the years by publicising the role and importance of exports in the economy and in nation building.

Minimum export policy consensus among different political parties to be arrived at to avoid constant changes in policies along with change of government, especially in view of the possibility of coalition governments at the centre.

Export Expertise and professionalism in export to be developed jointly by export organisations, business associations, government departments (both central and state) as well as the academia. An institute of export as in UK and Australia would give professional status to specialists in export. Training facilities for managers, deputies and staff in export related activities would help inculcate an export ethos.

Having reviewed exports in the past, examined the present and gazed at the future, one is more concerned today and cautiously optimistic about the future of India's exports than ever before. Lessons of past experience should always be borne in mind and continued self examination could lead us into the future with firm determination. Towards this, India should think in global terms, each of its citizens, contributing his share to export which alone could usher in a future India with its rightful place in the comity of nations - playing a role befitting its stature, reminiscent of the past.

9.2.3 CONCLUSIONS

The decreasing rate of growth in exports from 1996-97, combined with general downturn in world economy would call for more serious thought to be paid to India's export efforts. The IMF has predicted a slower rate of growth in India's exports (5.2%), as a result of weaker partner-country demand and infra-structure bottlenecks. The WTO has reversed its estimate of growth in world trade to 4% for 1998 and 3% for 1999, as a result of combination of factors starting from the Asian crisis and uncertainty of growth prospects in the EU and the USA. Despite slackening exports and its grim implications for foreign exchange reserves, export promotion does not find a place in any political parties' manifesto. Added to this there has been a decline in industrial activity, with members of the CII expressing a lack of 'feel good factor' and expecting a weakening of capital expenditure, production output and profit margins. The foreign exchange reserves of US$28B, would just cover import bills for a year, and should not lead to complacency. Exports need to be declared as a National Priority, and innovative export promotion strategies devised, if India is not to lose the gains from liberalisation of its economy.

Bibliography

Books and Periodicals

1. Asian Economic Focus, Lehman Brothers, 1994.
2. The Global Challenge, Oppurtunities and choices in the Multilateral trading system, Assocham Bulletin, December 1995.
3. Agosin, Manuel R., and Tussie Diana, (Eds.), Trade and Growth, London : The Macmillan Press Ltd., 1993.
4. Bhabatosh Datta, Indian Planning at the Crossroads, Delhi: Oxford University Press, 1992.
5. Business Asia - 20.11.95. Two Year Economic Outlook; India.
6. Bhagawati, Jagdish and Srinivasan T.N., India's Economic Reforms, New Delhi : The Associated Chambers of Commerce and Industry of India, 1993.
7. Cavusgil S. Tanner and Czinkota Michael. R. eds., International Perspectives on Trade Promotion and Assistance, Connecticut (USA) : Quorum Books, 1990.
8. Chawla R.L. ed., Development Co-operation for Strengthening International Economic Relations : India, Germany, EC and Japan. Indian Council for Research on International Economic Relations, New Delhi, 1992.
9. Choksi Armeane M., Papageorgiou Demetris, Economic Liberalisation in Developing Countries, Oxford, Blackwell, 1986.
10. Czinkota, Michael R., Tesar George eds. Export Policy: A Global Assessment, New York, Praeger, 1982.
11. Czinkota, Michael R., *et al.* eds., Export Promotion, The Public and Private sector interaction, New York, Praeger, 1983.

12. Dickie, Robert B., Layman Thomas A., Foreign Investment and Government Policy in the Third World, Basingstoke, Macmillan, 1988.

13. Devries, Barend A., Export Promotion Policies, Washington D.C. World Bank, 1979.

14. Export-Import Bank of India—13th Annual Report, 1994-95.

15. Export—Import Bank of India, "Come, Tap the Potential; India's new industrial and trade policy", October 1992.

16. Focus, WTO, Newsletter No.10, May 1996.

17. Global Emerging Markets—Equity Strategy, Lehman Brothers, 1995.

18. Guha Ashok, ed. Economic Liberalisation, Industrial Structure and Growth in India Delhi, Oxford University Press, 1990.

19. Dr. Harilela - Seminar on Hong Kong and India, Building a dynamic partnership, Hong Kong Trade Development Council, May 1995.

20. International Trade Centre, UNCTAD/GATT, Manual of Export Promotion Techniques(s.n.), New Delhi, 1973.

21. Lee Eddy, ed., Export Led Industrialisation and Development, Geneva, I.L.O., 1981.

22. Lall, Sanjaya, and Streeten, Paul, Foreign Investment, Transnationals and Developing Countries, London, Macmillan, 1977.

23. Jean Judith, M., Desai Seema and Ridel James, Trade Policy Reforms in Developing Countries, USA (Washington D.C.): The World Bank, 1994.

24. Das Dilip K., Emerging Growth Pole—The Asia Pacific Economy, Singapore : Prentice Hall, 1996.

25. Fontaine Jean-Marc ed., Foreign trade reforms and development strategy, New York : Routeledge, 1992.

26. Frazier Michael, Implementing State Government Export Programs, U.S.A: Praeger Publishers, 1992.

27. Grubel G. Herbert, Liberalisation of Trade in Services — A Taxonomy and Discussion of Issues, Singapore: Institute of South East Asian Studies, 1989.

28. Hughes Helen, ed., The Dangers of Export Pessimism. Developing Countries and Industrial Markets. USA (California) : International Centre for Economic Growth, 1992.

29. Herderschee Han, Incentives for Exports, A case study of Taiwan and Thailand, 1952-87, England: Avebury- Ashgate Publishing Ltd.,1995.

30. Imada Pearl, Naya Seiji, AFTA. The Way Ahead, Singapore: Institute of Southeast Asian Studies, 1992.

31. Jalan Bimal ed., The Indian Economy , Problems and Prospects, New Delhi: Penguin Books India (P) Ltd., 1992.

32. Krager Horst, Zimmerman F. Klaus, Export Activity and Strategic Trade Policy, Berlin: Springer - Verlag, 1992.

33. Macdonald Stuart, Technology and the Tyranny of Export Controls, New York: St. Martin's Press.

34. Market Report On India, Hong Kong Trade Development Council Research Department, Hong Kong, 1994.

35. McFetridge D., ed. Foreign Investment, Technology and Economic Growth, Calgary Alberta, University of Calgary Press, 1990.

36. Maizels Alfred, Export and Economic Growth of Developing Countries, New York : Cambridge University Press, 1971.

37. Milner, Chris ed., Export Promotion Strategies, Theory and Evidence from Developing Countries, Hertfordshire (London); Harvester Wheatsheaf, 1990.

38. Michaely Michael, Papageorgiou Demetris and Armeane M. Choksi eds. Liberalising Foreign Trade, USA (Massachusetts) Basil Blackwell Inc., 1991.

39. Nabhi's How To Export, New Delhi : Nabhi Publications, May 1995.

40. Nabhi's Supplement to New Import - Export Policy and Procedures, New Delhi : Nabhi Publications, August 1995.

41. Negandhi R. Anant, Peter Schran, eds. Research in International Business and International Relations, London : Jai Press Inc. 1990.

42. Negandhi R. Anant, International Management, USA (Massachusetts) : Allyn and Bacon Inc., 1987.

43. Ni. Sung-Shen, Causality between export and output growth: an empirical study of the relationship in Japan, South Korea, Taiwan, Hong Kong and Singapore, Ann Arbor, Michigan, University Micrefilms International, 1991.

44. Rhee Yung Whee and Belot Therese, Export Catalysts in Low Income Countries—A Review of Eleven Success Stories. USA (Washington D.C.) The World Bank, 1990.

45. Rana B. Pradumna, Changes in the Export Patterns of Asian and Pacific Developing Countries : An Empirical Overview, Philippines : The Asian Development Bank, 1987.

46. Ramachandran K.S., The Reform Process (An Evaluation), Delhi : Shipra Publications, 1995.

47. Ramdas P. Ganga, US Export Incentives and Investment Behaviour, Oxford : Westview Press.

48. Rao Chalapati K.S. and Dijck Pitou Van, India's Trade Policy and the Export Performance of Industry, New Delhi: Sage Publications, 1994.

49. Sarkar N.K., and Chattopadhyay, Boudhayan, Bombay, Orient Longman, 1976.

50. Seringhaus Rolf F.H. and Rosson J. Philip, Government Export Promotion : A Global Perspective, New York : Routelege, 1990.

51. Subramanian,S., ed., Themes in Development Economics, Essays in honour of Malcolm Audiseshiah, Delhi, Oxford University Press, 1992.

52. Twssoe, Diana and Glover David, eds., The Developing Countries in World Trade, Ottawa, International Trade Research Centre, 1993.

53. Whallez John, ed., Developing Countries and the Global

Trading System, Michigan, University of Michigan Press, 1992.

54. World Investment Report 1995. Transnational Corporations and Competitiveness (overview), United Nations; New York and Geneva, 1995.

55. World Development Report 1994, Infrastructure for development, USA (New York) Oxford University Press, 1994.

56. Tambunlertchai Somsak and Yamazawa Ippei. Manufactured Export Promotion - The Case of Thailand, Tokyo : The Institute of Developing Economies, 1983.

57. Varshney Roshanlal, India's Foreign Trade During and After the Second World War Allahabad : Kitab Mahal, 1954.

Journals

1. Asian Business
2. Asian Wall Street Journal
3. Arthavijnana
4. Business India
5. Business World
6. Business Week, USA
7. Business South Asia (EIU)
8. Economic and Political Weekly
9. Export (Institute of Export, UK)
10. Economist (London)
11. Economic Times (New Delhi)
12. Foreign Trade Review (IIFT, New Delhi)
13. Finance and Development (World Bank)
14. Foreign Trade-Trends and Tidings (IIFT)
15. Fortune
16. Forbes

17. IMF - Staff Papers
18. India Today
19. India Business
20. IMF, Annual Reports
21. OECD Publications
22. World Bank Reports
23. Yojana

Articles

1. APEC Set to Play Bigger Economic Role, South China Morning Post, Hong Kong 10.9.92.
2. Basic Statistics, India, CMIE, Aug. 1994
3. Business China Special Report, China and India—The Dragon and the Tiger, Seminar 1995.
4. The Bar is Lowered a few Notches, Anoop Jayram & Bhupesh Bhandari, Business World, Jan. 25, 1995.
5. Country Report, Pakistan, EIU—4th Quarter, 1995.
6. Contract Manufacturing in India, Quick, Cheap and Probably Wise, Business South Asia, Sep. 1995.
7. Consumer Goods—When Will the Walls Come Down? Business South Asia, Oct. 1994.
8. Chasing a Chimera - Pranjal Sharma, India Today, Feb. 15, 1996.
9. Can India Inc. keep up the Momentum? Business Week, Mar. 11, 1996.
10. Doubling Exports in Select Focus Product Groups by 1996-97, Backgrounder. Assocham, Aug. 14, 1993.
11. Dubey, Muchkund, Beyond the New Trade Order, New Delhi :The Economic Times, January 28th 1996.
12. Expansion Urged for Indian Ports, South China Morning Post, Hong Kong, 13th March, 1996.
13. East-Asia's Wobbles, The Economist, Jan. 5, 1996.

14. Export Performance, Recognising Reality, Surjit Bhalla, 1988.

15. Explaining the Service Sector Growth; An Empirical Study of India, Pakistan and Sri Lanka, Mohammed I. Ansari, Journal of Asian Economics, Volume 6, No. 2, 1995.

16. Economic Reform, India and Elsewhere, Lance Taylor, E & PW, Aug. 20, 1994.

17. Export Growth; Innovative Measures Urgently Needed, S.V. Sarkar, Statesman, Feb.2, 1993.

18. The Export Matrix :Whither Economic Diplomacy? K.M. Devarajan, Economic Times, Jan. 29, 1996.

19. Extreme Focus, Out of Focus, Economic Times, Jan. 19, 1996.

20. EXIM Policy and Procedures, Problem Areas and Some Suggestions, FICCI, Dec.15, 1995.

21. Extreme Focus Groups - An Update Foreign Trade - Trends and Tidings, Jul. 1995.

22. Export Strategy With a Focus on Country- Commodity - Matrix. Madan Lal, Foreign Trade - Trends & Tidings, Dec. 1995.

23. EXPORTS - Domestic Compulsions as Determinant, S. Chaudhury, Business Standard, Dec. 31, 1993.

24. Expansion urged for Indian ports, Agence France Presse, March 13, 1996.

25. Export-Import policy—Economic and Political Weekly, April 9, 1994.

26. Economic Indices - Our External Sector, Business India; May 8-21, 1995, p. 52.

27. Economic Indicators - Business World, 25.1.95.

28. G.S.P. changes hit Indian importers in EU, The Economic Times, Bombay, Dec. 26, 1994.

29. Enlarging the Indian Export Base by Antara Nanda, Observer, Feb. 16, 1994, p.6.

30. Economics of Import Substitution and Export Promotion

by T.S. Venkataraman, Financial Express, Nov. 16, 1993, p.7.

31. Export Promotion Stifled by Red Tape, by R.J. Venkataraman, Business Standard, Dec. 10, 1993, p.7.

32. Export Promotion; Why The Initiative may Flounder, by R.J. Venkateswaran, Business Standard, Dec. 22, 1993, p.7.

33. Export Promotion, Issues and Options, by R.N. Mishra, Business Standard, Sep. 28, 1993, p.7.

34. Export Promotion, Surviving in a Polarised Market, by R.N. Mishra, Business Standard, Sep.29, 1993, p.7.

35. Export Promotion : Co-ordinated Approach is the Key, by R.J. Venkateswaran, Business Standard, Feb.9, 1993, p.7.

36. Export Promotion; Centre and States should co-operate, by R.J. Venkateswaran, Business Standard, Feb.9, 1993, p.7.

37. Export Promotion ; Quantum Jump needed to Curb Trade Deficit, by S.B. Sarkar, Business Standard, Jul. 24, 1992, p.7.

38. *Export : Resilient Growth*, Pranjal Sharma, India Today, Jun 15, 1995.

39. EXIM Policy of India, Dr. Narayan Datt, IIFT, Jul. 94,

40. EXIT Policy - Need for a Pragmatic Approach, S. Ramakrishna, IIFT, 1993.

41. Foreign Trade Monthly Review CMIE, Dec. 1995.

42. GSP Changes Hit Indian Importers in E.U. H.N. Hebbar, Economic Times, 26, Dec. 1994.

43. Get on With the Programme, Nigel Holloway, Far East Economic Review, Jun 1, 1995.

44. GATT and Indian Services, Dr. P. Chattopadhyay, World Trade Review, July, 1994.

45. Global Challenge; Opportunities and Choices in the Multilateral Trading System, Assocham Bulletin, Dec. 1995.

46. The Garment Industry, Selling Inside and Out, Business South Asia, Nov. 1994.

47. Garment Exports, Nasima H. Khan, Economic Times, Dec. 5, 1994.

48. Gupta, Deepak - Indian Industry; small scale has not fared well, Business Standard, January 3, 1992.

49. Gearing up for Exports, by L.C. Jain, Economic Times, Aug.3, 1995, p.6.

50. How Competitive are Indian Industries? T.V.S. Shastri, Hindu Business Review, Sep. 13, 1995.

51. Hong Kong Economic Mission to India, Exporter's Bulletin, July, 1995.

52. Is This the Finance Ministry's Export Promotion Effort? IMPEX Times, July 25, 1995, p. 5.

53. India Simplifies Export Promotion, by K.K. Sharma, Financial Times, Jul. 27, 1990, p.4.

54. India : Economic outlook, 1995-97, Economic and Political Weekly, September 23, 1995.

55. India - Economic Outlook, 1995-97, Institute of Economic Growth and Delhi School of Economics, E&PW, Sep. 23, 1995.

56. Indian Economy, 1995-96 to 1997-98, Alternative Scenarios, K. Krishnamurthy, *et al.*, E&PW, Mar. 16,1996.

57. Indian Exports: A Race for Place, Kalyan Bannerjee, Economic Times, September 4, 1990.

58. India's Exports—Problems and Prospects, Sudip Bhattacharyya, Economic Times, September 29, 1989.

59. India's Export Opportunities in South Africa, D.S. Arora, Foreign Trade - Trends & Tidings, Jan. 1996.

60. India's Trade Relations with Central Asian Republics. Madan Lal, Foreign Trade - Trends & Tidings, Oct. 1995.

61. India's Trade and Investment Relations with Malaysia, Madan Lal, Foreign Trade - Trends & Tidings, Sep. 1995.

62. India Gains From GATT Accord, Kamala Suri, World Trade Review, May 1994.

63. India's Ability to Capture Benefits of R&D. Nirmal Kumar

Chandra, Economic & Political Weekly, Bombay, Jan. 22, 1994.

64. Impact of Real Exchange Rate—Movements on Selected Indian Industrial Products, Indira Rajavanan, Economic & Political Weekly, Mar. 1991.

65. India's Exports to Russia, R.G. Gidahubli, Economic & Political Weekly, Bombay, Nov. 4, 1995.

66. India's Emerging Priorities, Business India, Feb. 13, 1994.

67. Improve Infrastructure for Expert Expansion, D.R. Ahuja, Observer, Jul. 14, 1993.

68. India : Better than China? International Business, January 1995.

69. Looking out From London, Bhupesh Bhandari, Business World, Oct. 3, 1995.

70. Liberalisation. How Succesful? Y.C. Halan, Financial Express, Oct. 23, 1992.

71. Liberalisation in Trade, Industrial and Public Sectors in India, Dr. Tarun Kanthi Das, 1992.

72. Liberalisation Policy Irreversible, Dr. A. Ranga Ready, Financial Express, Nov. 25, 1993.

73. Lessons in Export Promotion, by A. Vijay Shekar, Financial Express, Mar. 1, 1991, p.6.

74. Liberation and Foreign Trade, Danger Signals, Economic & Political Weekly, May 4, 1996.

75. Liberalisation, Innovation and Exports, Rajat Acharyya, Economic & Political Weekly, Sep. 9, 1995.

76. Market report on India: Hong Kong Trade Development Council Research Department, Hong Kong, 1994.

77. Minister calls for South Asia Trade Zone, Economic Times, Jan. 27, 1993.

78. Manmohan Advocates Free Entry of Consumer Goods, Economic Times, Jan. 17, 1990.

79. Manufactured Exports and Newly Industrialising

Countries, Nigel Harris, Economic & Political Weekly, Mar. 1991.

80. Management Consultancy Comes Into it's own, R.J. Rajendraprasad, Hindu, Aug. 18, 1994.

81. Management of Development in the Newly Emerging Global Economic Environment, T. Krishnakumar, Economic & Political Weekly, Jun. 22, 1996.

82. Protection and Exports by Aditya Bhattacharya, Economic and Political Weekly, Sep.2, 1995, p. 2208-90.

83. Promoting or Impeding Exports? (Ed.), Financial Express, Oct. 6, 1993, p.6.

84. Purohit, C. Mahesh, Reform of Union Excise duties, Economic and Political Weekly, May 27, 1995.

85. Piercing the Bamboo Curtain, Latha Jishnu, Business World, Oct. 17, 1995.

86. Planning Reforms in Indian Economy, T.S. Venkataraman, Financial Express, Nov. 25, 1993.

87. Path to Excellence, S. Arunkumar & Vivek Khanna, Economic Times, Dec. 12, 1994.

88. Overview of World Trade, WTO—Focus Newsletter, May 1996.

89. Strategy for Sustainability of India's Export Growth, Backgrounder-ASSOCHAM, Oct. 20, 1994.

90. Stuck Between Two Worlds, Pankaj Ghemawat, Global, Oct. 1994.

91. SAARC ministers concentrate on co-ordinating Trade Flows, Arun Goyal, Economic Times, Jan. 15, 1996.

92. SAARC Summit -Trade Bonding, India Today, May 11, 1995.

93. Trading and Business Opportunities, A. Palkhivala, Assocham, Feb. 17, 1995.

94. Toward the Pacific age, James Walsh, Time, Nov. 22, 1993.

95. Tracking the Indian Economy, New Delhi, The Weekend Observer, January 27, 1996.

96. Two Year Economic Outlook- India, EIU, Business Asia, Nov. 20, 1995.

97. Unfinshed Task, Anjan Roy, Business India, Apr. 7, 1996.

98. Understanding the East - Asian Miracle, V.V. Bhatt, Review Economic & Political Weekly, Feb. 1994.

Index

	Name	*Pop.*	*Labour*	*Capital*	*Natural Resources*
1	China-Burma-Laos-Thailand (Golden Quadrangle)	47m	Thailand, Yunnan	Thailand	Laos, Burma
2	Indonesia-Malaysia-Thailand (Growth Triangle)	22m	Northern Sumatra	Penang	Southern Thailand
3	Indonesia-Malaysia-Singapore (Growth Triangle)	5.3m	Batam/Johor (limited)	Singapore	
4.	Southern China (Growth Triangle)	88m	Guangdong	Hong Kong and Taipei	Limited
5.	East ASEAN (Growth Polygon)	40m	All except Brunei	Brunei	All